EVERYDAY
DISCERNMENT

EVERYDAY DISCERNMENT

THE ART OF CULTIVATING
SPIRIT-LED LEADERSHIP

GREGG CHENOWETH

THE FOUNDRY
PUBLISHING®

Copyright © 2021 by Gregg Chenoweth
The Foundry Publishing®
PO Box 419527
Kansas City, MO 64141
thefoundrypublishing.com

978-0-8341-4063-9

Printed in the
United States of America

Cover design: Brandon Hill
Interior design: Sharon Page

Library of Congress Cataloging-in-Publication Data
A complete catalog record for this book is available from the Library of Congress.

The internet addresses, email addresses, and phone numbers in this book are accurate at the time of publication. They are provided as a resource. The Foundry Publishing does not endorse them or vouch for their content or permanence.

10 9 8 7 6 5 4 3 2 1

To my granddaughters, Audrey and Emmy, and their siblings and cousins to come. An inheritance would put something in your hand, but a family can do something even better—get a legacy in your heart. Maybe God will use these pages to awaken the SMG within you, for your benefit and the benefit of the generation you influence.

❈

Deuteronomy 4:9: Only be careful, and watch yourselves closely so that you do not forget the things you have seen or let them fade from your heart as long as you live. Teach them to your children and to their children after them.

CONTENTS

ONE
STEWARD THE MYSTERIES

A Mystery That Matters

God did something. But I didn't know it was God until much later.

We raised funds for a year to launch a debt-free college program. Families desperately need it. Bubbling with enthusiasm, I recruited a part-time program director. We knew the guy. His enthusiasm matched ours.

The thrill surged further when I met the first cohort of twenty students. One gal literally moved out of a homeless shelter and into a freshman dormitory. I could already imagine her as a thirty-five-year-old, looking back on the transformative years when she was being equipped for her robust career and discipled deeply in the faith, preparing for an escape from multigenerational poverty.

Then it happened. Only a few months after our launch, the program director resigned. *What?!* He didn't just change jobs but industries. So we replaced him with a new director who quit after just ten months. She disliked her supervisor because he held her accountable. Now get this: we hired the next guy, but after a week we discovered that he had deceived us during interviews, so we terminated him.

How is that for an inglorious beginning? If you're counting, we needed a fourth director after just eighteen months. The program was held together by duct tape, and it was vulnerable. The students deserved more stability, and I felt immense pressure to deliver for the generous donors who had placed $500,000 worth of their trust in us.

We needed supernatural intervention. So the vice president and I set aside the entire day of June 5—the date will be important later—for a fasting and prayer retreat, begging God to save this program, support these students, and *send* us a director we didn't recruit. Our premise was that God can accomplish more and faster than we can by ordinary means.

June 5 wasn't goofy. We didn't sacrifice any chickens or dance around a fire pit. We simply prayed (both corporately and alone), walked and talked, and asked the Holy Spirit to bring scriptures to mind that related to our dilemma. We read and reread, discussed, and decoded their meanings. We fasted too. Fasting isn't a fad diet but a demonstration to God and reminder to ourselves that the most important stuff of life becomes clear when we do not live by bread alone but by the Word of God (see Deut. 8:3; Matt. 4:4). Food denial becomes self-denial because our flesh cries out its demand all day long to be enthroned over every other concern. Fasting says no to King Stomach and yes to the Spirit. I find intense clarity by fasting in prayer.

Indeed, scriptures of particular timeliness came. We found ourselves in Exodus 35, where God summons Bezalel and Oholiab to particular jobs for which they are unusually gifted. First Kings 19 also resonated with us, where Elijah hears from God in a whisper. And what task does God assign Elijah with that gentle voice? A Human Resources mission. Elijah leaves God to appoint priests. We also spent time in Genesis 24, where a servant of Abraham looks for a wife for his son Isaac. Verse 15 jumped off the page at us: "Before he had finished praying, Rebekah came out [to the well] with her jar on her shoulder."

We turned these scriptures into our prayer, all day, in different ways. "God," we pled, "we see how you summon people to particular jobs, whisper names to hire, and sometimes answer *during* the asking. We believe you can do the same for us, for your glory."

I was stunned. Just twelve days later, we hired Rashad, whose credentials and impact exceeded his three predecessors.

Upon his arrival to our workplace, my curiosity oozed into conversation. At a welcome lunch, I said, "I want to tell you a story, but before I do, I have a strange question. Does June 5 mean anything to you?" He squinted, and I thought, *What a silly question. Who knows their own calendar like that?*

Then he said, "Actually, yes!" Thumbing through the calendar on his phone, he continued, "On June 5, I met a person who contacted me through LinkedIn. I didn't know her. But it's funny, we met to talk about something else, and ended up talking a lot about this university. Turns out, she'd sent her daughter here, loved it, and told me to look into it." And so he did, and here we are. Before Abraham's servant had even finished praying . . .

That is mysterious. But to a person in need of God, it is a mystery that matters.

Steward the Mystery

You might already be competent on the job or at home, maybe even titled with stature or well on your way there—but you picked up this book for a reason. Maybe you read that story about Rashad, and something stirred inside because you need God like that. Maybe you lack experience with, or are suspicious of, a Spirit-led life in your everyday projects—but you're curious.

I'm writing to folks who yearn to develop what the apostle Paul calls "competence" in matters of the Spirit (2 Cor. 3:5)—or, to put it another way, a faculty for discerning the leading of God. We are going to explore remarkable guidance across what may appear to be mundane experiences because most people are more familiar with Scripture than with the Holy Spirit. As Craig Keener explains in his book *The Mind of the Spirit*, "We are trained to solve problems with our own minds, trying to transform ourselves by beliefs. But we should recognize our dependence on the agency of God, the Spirit. Contrary to what our training leads us to expect, this experience comes not from wrestling with the idea of the Spirit, but entrusting ourselves to the One who gives us the Spirit."[1]

Learning tips, studying wisdom literature, figuring out what to do or what not to do—this all misses the point. You must move beyond intellectual analysis and actually engage with the Spirit. Paul contrasts this Spirit-led lifestyle of revelation and relationship with a focus on the letter of the law alone, that legalistic form of religion that promotes unreflective, rote behaviors. In Paul's time, for example, the hope to achieve righteousness by the rite of circumcision is off base: "Mark my words! I, Paul, tell you that if you let yourselves be circumcised, Christ will be of no value to you at all. Again I declare to every man who lets himself be circumcised that he is obligated to obey the whole law. . . . But if you are led by the Spirit, you are not under the law. . . . Since we live by the spirit, let us keep in step with the Spirit" (Gal. 5:2–3, 18, 25).

Performative obedience is not contrary to God's guidance—but it is incomplete. Across Romans 6–8, Paul helps the church in Rome understand that the law doesn't *solve* our sin problem—it only *reveals* it to us. When one realizes one is adrift from God, new behavior is necessary because who changes teams without wearing a new jersey? But merely putting on the jersey—though it is the correct way to begin—is performative obedience, not internal allegiance. Paul explains this to the new Christians in Rome who face several layers of behavioral demands from religious and civic leaders. He differentiates flesh (wearing the new jersey) from spirit (inward allegiance). "You, however, are not in the realm of the flesh but are in the realm of the Spirit, if indeed the Spirit of God lives in you. . . . For if you live according to the flesh, you will die; but if by the Spirit you put to death the misdeeds of the body, you will live" (Rom. 8:9a, 13).

If you want to develop a Spirit-led life, Paul is a good model. Like us, he never met Jesus materially but had to form intimacy with him spiritually. God profoundly changed Paul, and can change us too. We understand that we've been born into the faith, for "the Spirit himself testifies with our spirit that we are God's children" (Rom. 8:16). Something real and authentic happened, and keeps happening. While seeking him, you felt sought. In fact, Paul's spiritual transformation affected his very identity, telling people, "This, then, is how you ought to regard us: as servants of Christ and as those entrusted with the mysteries God has revealed" (1 Cor. 4:1).

I'll show instead of tell you. Imagine you're on a break between seminars at a professional conference. The lobby at the conference center offers coffee. You spot Paul in line, and his reputation precedes him. Your eyes meet, and there is a signal of mutual interest in greeting each other. Without any relational history, you know the conversational dance that is about to come: your names, where you're from, and then, of course: "So what do you do?" He slides a business card out of his wallet. You reciprocate. When you look down at Paul's card, you are surprised. The text on it doesn't reflect your expectation. This Billy-Graham-of-his-time hasn't called himself the "executive director of the Mideast evangelism initiative." It doesn't say CEO or executive vice president. It says "Paul, SMG." And he's asking you to consider him a steward of the mysteries of God.

The actual Greek word Paul uses for "steward" in 1 Corinthians 4:1 is *oikonomos*, a word typically used to indicate the manager of a household, someone who has been entrusted with operational affairs. He assumes responsibility for aspects of our faith and facilitates them as needed. His process is "to make plain to everyone the administration of this mystery" (Eph. 3:9). Just as a financial investor stewards cash by buying and selling for gain, or a physician stewards pharmaceuticals in timely remedy, Paul is saying that he stewards something too—the mysteries of God.

But he's not talking about mysteries as secrets held only by prophets and camouflaged from ordinary believers. Paul writes to a people whose culture is flush with clandestine religions, groups that foster mystique around their insider-outsider boundaries. Think of modern-day Masons or Scientology. So, when Paul uses the word *mysterion*, he is indicating that what was hidden is now revealed. He contrasts life in the Spirit with those secret societies. He is saying, *Those folks leave you guessing, but not us! Seek and you'll find.*

Jesus said as much in Matthew 13, answering why he so often speaks in parables: "Because the knowledge of the secrets of the kingdom of heaven have been given to you, but not to them. Whoever has will be given more, and they will have an abundance. Whoever does not have, even what they have will be taken from them. This is why I speak to them in parables: 'Though seeing, they do not see; though hearing, they do not hear or understand'" (vv. 11–13).

Parables contain layers of mystery on purpose. They are designed to awaken curiosity and satisfy those who pursue. To steward the mysteries is not a taunting, torturous call to crack an unbreakable code. It's more like, if Christ's salvation is authentic in you, then so are the spiritual faculties necessary to discern the ways of God. Reader, you must catch this: you can have everyday discernment from a Spirit-led life!

There are what we might call capital-M Mysteries and lowercase-m mysteries of the faith. In 1 Corinthians 4, Paul is specifically talking about the capital-M Mysteries: (1) that Jesus's sacrifice on the cross puts us at peace with God, and (2) that salvation is available to everyone, not just Jews. Paul explains this shift to new Christians in Ephesus, saying that this mystery, "which was not made known to people in other generations, has now been revealed by the Spirit to God's holy apostles and prophets. This mystery is that through the gospel the Gentiles are heirs together with Israel, members together of one body, and sharers together in the promise in Christ Jesus" (Eph. 3:5–6). Who gets the full resources of God? Not just the Jews of Israel anymore but now also gentiles—all of us who enter relationship with God by faith (Rom. 3:21-24). Merely wearing the jersey just doesn't get it done.

One could infer, wrongly, that an array of additional biblical mysteries remain out of reach to us twenty-first-century progeny. But no. Our discipleship means practicing what biblical figures standardized for us. Paul says, "Follow my example, as I follow the example of Christ" (1 Cor. 11:1) and, "Keep your eyes on those who live as we do" (Phil. 3:17b). This instruction includes that we should discern and follow the guidance of the Spirit as he does (Acts 16:6; 20:23). These constitute many lowercase-m spiritual mysteries. Paul perceives all of life from the activity of the Spirit of God upon us. With the material Jesus ascended to heaven, the Scriptures and the Spirit lead us.

Look at it this way. Right now, as you hold this book in your hand, the air around you holds the ability to bring you mood-changing music. These songs do not announce themselves out of the air, however. You must seek them. Gliding across the air space of your room are invisible radio signals just waiting to bring you jazz, classical, rap, rock—whatever your taste. If only you possessed a frequency to download it, your mood—maybe your whole day—could be immediately changed! Siphon off Aerosmith's "Dream On" from the airwaves, and within minutes you might be playing air guitar. Download Jay Z's groove from the electromagnetic field, and involuntarily your head might bob. By radio waves that are shorter than a grain of rice, the technical torrent of Chopin's keyboard might elevate your spirit.

And there's more: you can't see it, but gliding across your ceiling are the incomprehensibly vast resources of the internet. Of course, you need a device to extract the whereabouts of Kim Kardashian or learn the World Cup rankings of your favorite soccer club, but it's all there, waiting to be found. I don't have to persuade you of this reality. The information is invisible, but it is real, immense, and effective. Yet, without the awareness to seek it or a way to access it, these unfathomably rich resources lie dormant in your life.

You see where I'm going, right? It's exactly the same with the Holy Spirit, only we're not talking about some*thing* but some*one*—an invisible, interested, responsive Person of the Trinity, of the same mind as God the Father and God the Son. But don't get it twisted. What we download has a particular purpose. This book isn't a health-and-wealth message to leverage a spiritual mystery for personal gain, like getting a lottery number from God. Material benefits surely come from the God who positions himself as father (Exod. 4:22–23) and provider (Gen. 22:14). But that's the frosting, not the cake. God's primary project is to make us holy, not healthy; wise, not wealthy; and sanctified, not generically successful. This book is about finding everyday discernment, getting remarkable guidance during what might appear to be mundane projects. I'm telling you, God guides!

Experience God Like Paul—Really?!

We must admit that, in many ways, Paul's life is a showpiece of unrepeatable particularities. I'll never become him—in the same way I'll never ascend to the Bench like Ruth Bader Ginsburg, or sell 650 million copies of imaginative wonder like Theodor Geisel (Dr. Seuss), or climb onto thirteen championship podiums like Phil Jackson. Theologically, we acknowledge that God selects certain people in particular times for extraordinary purposes. Ancient Israel carries more weight than Switzerland for signs from God; Moses and David get more ink in the holy writ than Naaman or Mordecai. Jesus atones for sin, and no other. Each of them bears unique, divine, historic necessity, and so it is the same with Paul.

In another respect, however, let's not be tempted to make Paul so angelic or alien as a superapostle that we could never imitate him. For starters, he didn't talk in thunder and dazzle with Hollywood charisma. The only physical description of Paul from an early church document, The Acts of Paul, said he was short, bald, bowlegged, long of nose, and had large eyes under what today we would call a unibrow![2] This characterization seems exaggerative, but Paul himself shares that it is corroborated by his critics: "For some say, 'His letters are weighty and forceful, but in person he is unimpressive and his speaking amounts to nothing'" (2 Cor. 10:10).

Paul didn't invent Christianity with insights no one else had, like some kind of new Moses, descending from a mountain after privately conferencing with God. Jerry Sumney demonstrates thoroughly in *Steward of God's Mysteries* that Paul was truly special as a spokesperson and missionary but not as a diviner of new things. He assembled and articulated beliefs that were already held across the regions to which he traveled. Sumney says we should reject an image of Paul as a hero, and understand instead that other formulators of early church doctrine informed *him*. "Their work as theologians come to us *through* the letters of Paul. . . . This clearly does not mean the revelation was to Paul alone or his revelation was different from the rest of the church. . . . [Paul's] genius is seen in the ways he is able to bring those beliefs into new environments" in a missional sense.[3]

But you're still thinking, *Yeah, but I'm no Paul!* Let's check on something. Is it possible you can't imagine stewarding mysteries of the faith because memory stole your imagination? Struggle can sap belief. Disappointment in or prolonged delays from God can breed doubt, which can leave you in a position of confirmation bias, believing in God's neglect then finding evidence for it around every turn. Such a person curates sour memories, like a museum of ugly art in the mind. Behind their eyes rests a dim resignation that God will never surprise them. He will never transcend their circumstance. Life is what it is. This is what A. W. Tozer describes in *The Knowledge of the Holy* as a person whose memory overtakes imagination.[4]

But there are others who, despite the same delays or disappointments in God, actively recall his faithful activity in their lives or the lives of others. In the museum of their minds hang breathtaking, technicolor scenes of testifiers with warm remembrance of God's faithfulness. Their eyes twinkle in anticipation for God's coming work. This kind of imagination can become extra-biblical—immature, wishful thinking, pie-in-the-sky silliness—but it doesn't have to be. Philip Eaton describes biblical imagination as eagerly awaiting promptings of the Holy Spirit, observing God's presence, not his absence, a winsome and evocative talk that is fully authorized in the face of those who dismiss. Great people and organizations are built on this kind of speech that shatters doubt. But it all starts with how we manage our memory. "Change," Eaton says, "is most enduring when it penetrates the structure of our imagination."[5]

Let's open up your imagination through a crash course on the Holy Spirit. There is not a person anywhere—of antiquity or modern time—who can assume Christian identity without the presence of the Holy Spirit. Even if your radar is dull to the reality, the Spirit is there (John 7:38–39; 1 Cor. 3:16), and provides sufficient power to live a life pleasing to God (Acts 1:8; Rom. 8:1–17; 2 Pet. 1:3). The Spirit counsels our conscience toward the deep things of God (1 Cor. 2:10). The Holy Spirit proceeded from God the Father (John 15:26), descended upon Jesus the Son at his baptism (Matthew 3:16; Mark 1:10; Luke 3:22; John 1:32), and—get this—even Jesus depended on the Spirit for power and to teach him what the Father wanted him to say (Luke 4:14; Acts 1:2). To this day, the Holy Spirit woos us to God (John 6:44); convicts us of sin (John 16:8); regenerates us in a new identity (Eph. 2:4); enables a fruitful and virtuous character (Gal. 5:22–33); bestows special abilities for service to the church (Rom. 12:3–8; 1 Cor. 12:4–11; Eph. 4:1–13); and teaches and reminds us of what we've been taught (John 14:26). The Holy Spirit is everywhere; we can't escape the Spirit's awareness (Ps. 139:7). The Holy Spirit is so important to Christian life that to deny and denounce the reality and work of the Spirit is a blasphemous, unforgivable sin (Matt. 12:30–32).

But any work attributed to the Spirit must be attached to Scripture. Many of us know the experience of an impression of mind while reading Scripture or praying, but that internal experience can only ever be called a perspective if it is not disciplined against the enduring authority of Scripture. As Henry and Richard Blackaby express it, "When God speaks, he does not give new revelation about himself that contradicts what he has already revealed in Scripture, but to reveal an application of his Word to the circumstances of your life."[6] Little wonder the apostle Paul mentions the Spirit 160 times in his epistles.

Now, a caveat. Stewarding mysteries of the faith is not tantamount to mysticism. Though many believers enjoy a beautiful and biblically sound heritage of Christian mystics, the definitions matter. Justin Taylor explains in *The Gospel Coalition* that Christian mystics perceive they actually experience direct, unmediated, complete unity with the divine, and are therefore illuminated with the capacity to see divine purpose purely.[7] But evangelical spirituality recognizes distance between God as a holy other and the seeker as God's subject who cannot generate their own encounter with God. Mysticism emphasizes God's presence in everything (immanence) while evangelicalism emphasizes God's separateness (transcendence). Therefore, God reaches toward me and directs me, but I do not have God's mind infallibly. My experience is interpreted and therefore falsifiable, if not grounded in Scripture.

Therefore, a spiritual practice we disparage is sensationalistic, manufactured emotion, an almost pantheistic trait in locating spiritual agency behind every conversation, billboard, or political development. You could Google titles of books to assist you in that domain if you like: explorations of the hidden messages in nature, numerology, dream analysis, the surreal power of mystic places, or the utility of crystals. That's not this book. Deep problems arrive quickly—terribly fractious problems that destroy marriages, families, and churches—when a person claims special knowledge of God that is unaccountable to Scripture or the counsel of a community of mature believers (1 Cor. 5:12–13; 14:29–33; 1 Thess. 5:19–22). I have witnessed this firsthand. An impression of mind that occurs while seeking encounter with God can be mistaken *for* God. Nowhere does the Bible indicate that Satan can read our thoughts, but Satan can certainly deceive a person into false confidence in their prophecy in order to wreak havoc in the church (1 Sam. 18:10–11). We ought not think our Christian status makes us impervious to this deception because Jesus himself faced challenges of mind by Satan in the desert. Notably, he disposed of those challenges by Scripture (see Matt.

4:1–11; Luke 4:1–13). This is why our ancestors in the faith admonish us to put on the full armor of God, in order to be protected from the fiery darts of the enemy (Eph. 6:10–18). We fight with "the sword of the Spirit, which is the word of God" (v. 17).

When the Bible commands us to test the spirits (1 Thess. 5:19–22; 1 John 4:1), it means we must cite the source of our spiritual impressions. We must not assume our thoughts carry the same authority as God. We aren't showing *greater* faith by speaking forcefully from our personal experience; that is *misplaced* faith in our own discernment.

The Identity-Action Link

Because we are indicated as new creatures in Christ, we follow the imperative to think and act differently. A few years ago, I took this quite seriously. I am a CEO, but I thought, *If my functional identity was SMG* (indicative), *how might I steward the mysteries of God* (imperative)? What difference could identity make in my behavior at work, at home, in my community, and in my friendships? I got so excited by the notion it became a devotional series with our executives. And, just for kicks, I changed the titles on our board meeting tent cards for myself and all VPs: not chief academic officer (CAO), but SMG for academics; not chief financial officer (CFO), but SMG for our finances. You get the picture.

Self-identity is abstract but uncomplicated. You are the constellation of the roles you play in life together with what you believe about yourself in playing those roles (e.g., father, leader, hobbyist, Christian, etc.). In order to get this text into your hands, I had to believe I am a writer. Without that belief, it doesn't get done. It works the same way in a negative sense. The transcript of our inner dialogue can awaken either faith *or* doubt, buoy confidence or sink hope, thrust you through to the other side of the most bitter hardships of life, or destroy you.

Therapists are paid large sums to help us understand it. A detached dad barks toward his teenage son that to be a man, more than anything else, is to provide financially. When that boy grows up and has a family, the provider identity bullies him into workaholism because he thinks the grind and the cash prove his love and care—but he it got twisted. As with almost all things, a strength becomes a weakness when you magnify it. So the workaholic succeeds in one dimension but fails miserably in another. He becomes an absentee husband whose wife's wrist sparkles in diamonds when what she most wants is someone to talk to at dinnertime. One day he wakes up divorced and totally baffled. An unchecked identity begat disastrous habits.

But the identity-behavior link can bring the best out of us too! I remember interviewing a midlevel staff person for promotion. Internal promotions can be tricky. One day your colleagues are your friends, and the next you're their boss, wielding the power of bonuses, terminations, gravy assignments or dreadful ones. That change in hierarchy is not a change in kind but degree—not doing more of the same thing but assuming an entirely new set of demands and accountabilities that affect your awareness, activity, and identity.

The interview surprised me.

"What have you been doing to prepare to become a director?" I asked her, rifling through the resumé. I'll never forget her answer.

"Maybe a year ago," she said, "I decided this will be the Year of Me."

I grinned. She got my attention. "What's that?" I asked.

Staring toward the ceiling, pensively, she began a confessional but empowering story.

"Well, to be honest, it occurred to me that I have expected too little of myself. Life was passing me by. I've been trapped in the daily grind, without motivation for something new or more. So I got a professional coach who helped me focus on goals. I decided that I really have it in me to be a director, but I hadn't been thinking or acting like it. I started looking at my work and the team as something I could be more responsible for. I volunteered for new projects. I became less sensitive to criticism. I initiated more. This entire process really opened up a new part of my life, and I like it!"

That intrigued me, but I wanted to check the depth of this new identity.

"You know, becoming director offers a lot of benefits but also some bitter responsibilities. Who is the lowest-performing person in the department, and under what criteria would you terminate their employment?"

She giggled nervously, acknowledging, "Well, I haven't spent any time thinking about that, but I know part of my job is to work early so that moment doesn't have to happen."

That was a great answer. A change of identity requires a change of behavior. We promoted her. She did well, leading the team into its height of influence and productivity. She really stepped up to make tough decisions, and it started with her internal dialogue that said, *I'm the director now.*

So when Paul says, *think of me like an SMG*, it is significant. And I want you to start thinking, *What if I were an SMG too?* How might that affect your attitudes, expectations, conversations, and behaviors? No matter your title for a workplace, college council, or team, if God's mind and power are as accessible as the internet or radio waves flowing through the air around you right now, what kind of clarity and focus are possible in the ambitions and projects of your life?

The Chapters Ahead

Because you are a person of influence, or aspire to be, you very likely already have a project or ambition in mind. You are coiled, ready to spring toward it, or at least want to prepare for such a moment. Imagine stewarding the mysteries of God throughout the process.

The coming chapters are organized around the standard phases of a generalized project. The Project Management Institute (PMI) began in 1969 and has become the largest nonprofit membership association for project managers.[8] Their taxonomy includes components such as conception, risk assessment, milestones, team members, resources and budgets, key performance indicators (KPIs), reporting, and postmortems. The chapters to come are loosely based on those phases, but because our focus is spiritual practice rather than management itself, we will exclude some PMI prompts that do not apply, and we will translate other phases to suit our purpose toward the spiritual vision of those who are in the seat of influence during a project. For example, conceiving of a project translates to a chapter about watching for signs of change; risk management converts to discerning when to start; reporting becomes more about coping with bad news and how to respond to hardship; budgets looks into the spiritual principle of generosity, especially when funds are limited.

Each chapter examines a spiritual mystery Paul had to discern that is relevant to that phase of project development. From this, we get equipped to steward that mystery ourselves. Note that we do not address biblical mysteries of such miraculous rarity—visions, healings, voices—that, while possible in our time, are not probable in the most common experience of Christian faith. The project phases and mysteries to steward include:

Chapter 2: While watching for signs of change, find remarkable guidance from what appear to be mundane experiences.

Chapter 3: While estimating the best time to start, discern God's delay from direction.

Chapter 4: When in need of collaborators for your cause, discover how God sends people you don't recruit who become to you Godsends.

Chapter 5: While managing money, experience how God returns your generosity.

Chapter 6: When facing conflict, yield godly sorrow and lasting peace from confrontation, not avoidance.

Chapter 7: When encountering hardship, become pleased by the purpose of your pain and enjoy the enduring power of God.

Chapter 8: Bear witness to Christ as you go, and see that God still saves by the foolishness of preaching.

Are you ready to practice everyday discernment as an SMG? Let's go.

TWO
WATCHING FOR SIGNS OF CHANGE

"It was the strangest, most wonderful, most astonishing time of my life."

That's how John Avant described giving up one dream for another while he and his wife, Donna, watched for signs of change. An unusual encounter with God inspired them to leave a church of eight thousand people they pastored in Knoxville, Tennessee, for an assignment five hundred miles away in Michigan. They were in their mid-fifties, with no established relationships where they were going, and no salary on offer!

Soak that in. The church they were leaving was a unicorn: believed to exist but never seen—at least by most. According to the National Congregations Study, of 400,000 churches in the United States, only 100 of them burst at the seams to that degree. To appreciate the Avants' risk of transition, imagine a gal goes into medicine, spends 12 years of formal education to specialize, rakes up $250,000 in debt, builds a practice of such acclaim that parents fly their newborns across the country to be in her care. Or, imagine another guy's entrepreneurial spark discovers a market niche, so he mortgages his home and liquidates retirement savings to start up, and twenty years later he owns a market share that is impervious to competitors.

So you'd be willing to leave that kind of success behind, right? No way—unless . . .

The Avants spoke at an event organized by the Billy Graham Training Center, during which they re-surrendered their lives to God at an altar. What they did not know was that some representatives of Life Action Ministries in southwestern Michigan were standing in the back of the same room. These representatives felt prompted to invite the Avants to lead their organization, a quiet yet powerful collection of three hundred people who raise their own support while they foster revival in small and large cities, on campuses, and at churches across the United States.

Despite John and Donna's unusual success in Knoxville, including love and support from their congregation and staff, the invitation came in a context of discontent. For several months, unhappiness had hovered that they didn't understand. It persisted long enough that they sought peace in the Scriptures, learning how great leaders of the faith—Elijah, David, Jeremiah, Paul—also became unbearably sad but found transformative and reorienting help in God.

A nagging issue was the wageless offer from Life Action. It scared them. But, during a hike into the mountains to read and pray, God directed their attention not only to his demand ("Whoever wants to be my disciple must deny themselves and take up their cross and follow me" [Matt. 16:24]) but also his deliverance, where the apostle John praises a wealthy friend for funding missionaries he doesn't even know ("Dear friend, you are faithful in what you are doing for the brothers and sisters, even though they are strangers to you" [3 John 1:5]). Hmm. Interesting timing.

Then something startling happened. John writes in their book:

I went out for an early morning run. A man dropped dead on the beach in front of me! His son shouted, "Can he be revived?" as I watched paramedics trying to save him.

After a while, I ran down the beach a mile more, but overwhelmed by emotion, I sat by a washed-out pier, wept, and sang. When I opened my eyes, a 75-year-old woman was standing in front of me. She had simply been resting on the other side of the pier. Smiling, she asked me, "Are you singing to the King of kings?"

"Yes," I said in shock.

"I have a word from him to you: *He's been with you everywhere you have been, and he will be with you where you are about to go.*"

I told her my whole story and the decision Donna and I had to make. She told me her husband lived in a condo that shared a wall with the one we were renting for the week, and said, "I'm sure you are ready to make your decision now to lead Life Action. After all, today you watched a man die who could not be revived, but there are people and churches everywhere who can be!"[1]

John and Donna experienced a mystery that matters: finding guidance through experiences. While they watched, God led. So John walked inside, picked up the phone, and accepted the position.

Finding Guidance through Experiences

God leads people who watch, ready for signs of change. Run instant replay on the Avants' story, and we can see a string of experiences—artifacts of life that may have appeared to have no spiritual purpose—that later become flooded with meaning. The restlessness had purpose; so did a conversation at a conference; Scripture came during a hike; an emotionally potent event on the beach led to an unknown woman with astonishing applicability; unity of judgment came between John, Donna, and others who affirmed Godward markers around their lives. Piece by piece, clarity comes, like discovering stars in the night sky, one after another, some brilliantly obvious, others subtly faint, until one day you realize they are part of a constellation.

Throughout Paul's writings, we are reminded there really is no distinction between sacred and secular experiences because there is no space where we escape God's presence. This does not mean God is acting in all of our experiences or perceptions. That assumption invites attribution errors, lending authority and agency to every billboard message or spontaneous conversation, when instead—as Craig Keener clarifies—for us to adopt the mind of the Spirit (Rom. 8:6) really means locating thoughts that are characteristic of God, not *every* fleeting thought. "Having the mind of Christ, or acting on the basis of one, provides: moral empowerment, a Christocentric and ecclesiastic missional framework of thinking, periodic personal direction from the

Spirit, periodic experiences of divine wisdom, periodic revelatory insights, and so on."[2]

So, by examining Paul's experiences, we might see whether our own stars are a constellation. He had unmistakably brilliant ones—miraculous events like healings, earthquakes, and visions. Let's call those Type I Guidance. Moderately bright stars appeared too, what we might call Type II Guidance—episodes seemingly *created* by God for Paul's direction: a group of people appointed Paul their leader following prayer; he often felt compelled to go to a city or to wait; he survived a lethal snake; and he discovered a well-placed companion to help him escape capture. Finally, we find dimmer stars, a Type III Guidance from what appear to be naturally occurring events made significant by supernatural insight. For Paul, it was a belt, rain, and joy despite suffering.

This nomenclature helps us rise above silly debates, like whether the dead man on the beach was Type I for John Avant. No, God did not kill a man to offer insight for John and Donna! It is easier to conclude that his death was Type III: God may have placed John in the right place and time to witness what was going to happen anyway, and it made an impact on his decision.

Indeed, mysteries need a steward! If God made a habit of writing messages in the sky for us, we wouldn't need this chapter. Because we are most often guided by a package of Type IIs and Type IIIs—the dimmer, more subtle stars—no wonder Paul describes a competence to discern the Spirit (2 Cor. 3:5-6). Despite how dim a star might be, God does guide. The question is not, "Will God guide us?" but, "Are we attentive enough to notice?"

Those without the Spirit can't get this. It is to them a preposterous mystery, unacceptable and foolish, total hogwash, the stuff of fairies and magical thinking (1 Cor. 2:14). In fact, sin itself blunts our capacity to hear from God—or him from us (Ps. 66:18). But the new or maturing believer has the Spirit of God. We talk and operate differently. "We do, however, speak a message of wisdom among the mature . . . God's wisdom, a mystery . . . God has revealed to us by his Spirit. . . . For who knows a person's thoughts except their own spirit within them? In the same way no one knows the thoughts of God except the Spirit of God. . . . We speak, not in words taught us by human wisdom but in words taught by the Spirit, explaining spiritual realities with Spirit-taught words" (1 Cor. 2:6a, 7b, 10a, 11, 13b). Therefore, I have no hope of reaching an unbeliever on this matter, but for a Christian, "We are not trying to commend ourselves to you again, but are giving you an opportunity to take pride in us, so that you can answer those who take pride in what is seen rather than in what is in the heart. If we are 'out of our mind,' as some say, it is for God; if we are in our right mind, it is for you" (2 Cor. 5:12–13).

C. S. Lewis explains the difference between Christian miracles and mythological ones, like fairy tales where animals turn into people or trees talk: "[Miracles] are what might be expected to happen when earth is invaded not simply by a god, but by the God of Nature," who can bend what he designed.[3] We tend to focus on extraordinary episodes without wonder for the marvels right under our feet:

> Every year, as part of the natural order, God makes wine. He does so by creating a vegetable organism that can turn water, soil, and sunlight into a juice which will, under proper conditions, become wine. Thus, in a certain sense, he constantly turns water into wine. Once, [referring to Jesus's first miracle in John 2] God short-circuits the process, makes wine in a moment, uses earthenware jars instead of vegetable fibers to hold the water, but uses them to do what he is always doing. The miracle consists in the shortcut, but the event to which it leads is the usual one.[4]

This means we must train our eyes to see God's activity more clearly. Leonard Sweet counsels us in *Nudge* that Christians often believe more in omnipresent evil than an omnipresent God.[5] We think of God *in* the garden, Jesus *in* heaven, and the Spirit *in* our hearts, instead of imagining God acting in our time. Diagnosing the artifacts of our lives for sacred content isn't manufacturing a hopeful illusion. God is already here. Our task is to discern what is he saying to us.

God is a master semiotician. Semiotics is the study of signs—anything from symbols to metaphors. The subspecialties are semantics (the relation of signs to how they are interpreted, such as connotations) and pragmatics (the effect signs have on us). Remember the various signs set between God and his people, and marvel at their pragmatic effects: the rainbow, circumcision, following God throughout the exodus under a cloud and behind a pillar of fire, a star in the east, a manger, the cross. These are all signs.

To be sure, Jesus condemns those who demand signs (see Matt. 16:4; Mark 8:12) because they become idols to feed our craven appetite. The point of watchfulness is not the sign but coming into step with the Sign Giver. If, while driving to Chicago, you see a sign that says "Chicago: 60 miles," you don't pull over and admire it. Instead, that sign confirms that you are on the right track, and you might even accelerate your pace toward the destination from the confidence that sign gives you.

Those who believe they serve a God who speaks will build a spiritual acuity for watchfulness that does not exist in many believers. But once we can distinguish valuable, transcendent signs from white noise, we can discover what Paul describes as walking by the Spirit (Gal. 5:16)—a lifestyle of God-consciousness. Jesus describes it as discerning wind—invisible, yes, but you hear the sound. "So it is with everyone born of the Spirit" (John 3:8b; see vv. 5–8).

The Lord says to one in need of guidance, "Call to me and I will answer you and tell you great and unsearchable things you do not know" (Jer. 33:3). Jesus assures us the Speaker can be heard—"My sheep listen to my voice; I know them, and they follow me" (John 10:27)—and that more is to come: "I have much more to say to you, more than you can now bear. But when he, the Spirit of truth, comes, he will guide you into all the truth. He will not speak on his own; he will speak only what he hears" (John 16:12–13). The posture we should take is like Habakkuk, who said, "I will stand at my watch and station myself on the ramparts; I will look to see what he will say to me" (2:1a).

Three Methods to Test Interpretation of Experiences

We learn from Paul how to interpret remarkable guidance from what some might believe is mundane experience: by Scripture, prayer, and confirmation from mature believers.

First, Scripture guides most reliably. Paul digs in. He is a Pharisee trained by Gamaliel (Acts 22:3)—a man whose guardianship over Scripture and judgment about it was so respected he had the social power to persuade the entire Sanhedrin (see Acts 5:34). Even after such intense Jewish training, Paul followed his conversion to Christ with another three years of study (see Gal. 1:15–20). Read through his epistles and note how frequently he quotes the Hebrew Scriptures! Little wonder he instructs churches to "devote yourself to the public reading of Scripture" (1 Tim. 4:13) and to "watch your life and doctrine closely" (v. 16). Scripture equips us for "every good work" (2 Tim. 3:17).

Paul knows, as we do, that the Holy Spirit inspired the writing of Scripture and has safeguarded it to this day from doctrinal corruption during language translations. From it we learn how to reconcile ourselves to God, and everything else necessary for living a God-honoring life (2 Peter 1:3–4). In it we see God's character, his patterns of judgment, and how he guided our ancestors in the faith. If you ever doubt whether you are praying in God's will, pray from Scripture. If you doubt your decisions or actions, find sanction in Scripture. If you don't know what to pray, read Scripture until the Spirit prompts something for you to pray about.

Second, a lifestyle of prayer also equips us to discern God's guidance. In prayer, we cultivate spiritual listening, heighten our consciousness of God, and do not strain to hear God but remain open for insight. We quiet our inner dialogue—so often full of emotional and psychological noise, confusion, anxiety, and unrest—and eventually sink beyond our thoughts and into his.

On one hand, when we want to tell God things, we have confidence that God draws near to us every time we pray (Deut. 4:7), and he listens to the righteous even as he remains against those who do evil (1 Pet. 3:12). Paul practices what he preaches: to "pray continually" (1 Thess. 5:17), sometimes in serious, "wrestling" prayer (Col. 4:12); begging God to remove a nagging struggle (2 Cor. 12:7–9); asking God to open up opportunities (1 Cor. 16:9; 2 Cor. 2:12; Col. 4:3); seeking rescue (Rom. 15:30–33), and many other ways.

On the other hand, in prayer we also have the opportunity to hear from God. Notably, Paul also prays that God would give us "the spirit of wisdom and revelation, so that you may know him better" (Eph. 1:17b). This revelation comes from God speaking to us. Jesus says that "when he, the Spirit of truth, comes, he will guide you into all the truth" (John 16:13a), and Paul affirms that whoever sows the Spirit reaps the Spirit (Gal. 6:8).

In prayer we often experience an impression of mind that can be attributed to God when linked to Scripture. The Holy Spirit reminds us what we have already been taught so that we can apply it to the circumstance over which we pray (John 14:26). This is why Jesus calls the Holy Spirit the "Advocate" and "Counselor."

Third, we will more accurately discern God's guidance when mature believers agree with our interpretation. Luke reports that the Jerusalem council wrote to gentile believers, "It seemed good to the Holy Spirit *and to us*" (see Acts 15:28, emphasis added). And, later, "after Paul had seen the vision, *we got ready at once* to leave for Macedonia, *concluding that God had called us* to preach the gospel to them" (Acts 16:10). Confirmation from others is common sense because isolated experience is inherently interpreted by one person and is only mediated through the limitations of our own knowledge. We call individual experience "perspective," which cannot carry more authority than Scripture or the common experience of many mature believers. It is best if we do this together, conferring and agreeing about what God is doing.

Ruth Haley Barton says in *Pursuing God's Will Together*, "As inspiring as the idea of teamwork is, it falls short of what Christians are called to be: to move beyond teamwork and live into that great spiritual reality called Christian community."[6] If the question is how to prepare to be led by God, then the answer is, in unity. Unity is the fundamental marker of the activity of the Spirit. As the Psalmist said, "How good and pleasant it is when God's people live together in unity! For there the LORD bestows his blessing" (Ps. 133:1, 3b). The complexity and confusion of our lives is perfectly met by the Holy Spirit, who helps us interpret the deep things of God (1 Cor 2:10).

Now, let's look back into Paul's experiences to see how Types I, II, and III created a constellation of stars to guide him. The brightest, most easily identified acts of God are Type I: extraordinary miracles. In Acts alone, Paul:

- hears a voice of guidance (9:1–9);
- blinds an enemy (13:9–11);
- heals a lame man (14:8–10);
- has visions from the Lord (16:6–10; 18:9–11; 22:17–21);
- exorcises a demon (16:16–18);

- is released from prison by earthquake (16:25–36);
- causes twelve people to prophesy in the Spirit after touching them (19:6–7);
- cures illnesses by touching handkerchiefs (19:11–12);
- raises a dead man to life (20:9–12);
- receives a revelation from an angel foretelling that lives will be spared during a crisis at sea (27:21–44);
- heals a person of dysentery (28:7–8).

Among many others, let's not forget the miracle it is when throngs of people come to Christ for salvation as Paul preaches the gospel. Look at that list and it is easy to conclude: God guides!

But Paul also experiences dimmer stars, Type II experiences that appear to be created by God for our guidance. In Acts alone:

- the prophets and teachers at the church in Antioch fast and pray then tell Paul they believe God wants him to work with Barnabas, so Paul does (13:1–3);
- despite persecution, Paul feels joy as affirmation of his new ministry (13:49–52);
- he survives a stoning (14:19–20);
- Paul and his missionary companions are "kept by the Holy Spirit from preaching" in multiple cities, for "the Spirit of Jesus would not allow them to" (16:6–7);
- he is "compelled by the Spirit" to go to Jerusalem (20:22);
- the Spirit working through others later delays his departure (21:4);
- he senses the Lord's presence with him in prison (23:11);
- when he handles a lethal snake without injury, those who witness it change their minds about Paul's message (28:1–6).

There is also a subtlety of Type III stars in the constellation, naturally occurring experiences made significant with supernatural meaning. In the book of Acts alone:

- rain is interpreted as a kindness from God (14:17);
- Paul eludes political actions to entrap him (17:5–9);

- Paul finds favor with Roman rulers, who release him from charges (18:12–16);

- people burn their sorcery books in response to his preaching (19:13–20);

- a belt takes on prophetic meaning (21:11);

- a well-positioned companion learns secret information that saves his life (23:16);

- Paul's willingness to be martyred is an unnatural, or supernatural, conviction (25:10–11).

Taken together, Types I, II, and III leave us convinced that God guided Paul. He guides us too. But don't make the mistake of watching only for Type I in your life. You might never experience that. For centuries, debates have raged over whether signs and wonders were confined by God to the original apostles (cessationism), or extend to the contemporary era (continuationism). Even the popular pastor, writer, and continuationist John Piper confesses an unresolved inner conflict on this question, making the case for each side in *Desiring God*.[7]

Upholding the case for cessationism include the arguments that:

(1) they were extraordinary symbols used to validate the authority of Jesus and his apostles in their time in order that we might read them as authorities today (Acts 2:22, 43; 14:3; Rom. 15:17–19);

(2) even in the New Testament era, signs and wonders were often described as prior events used to testify to the salvation message of Christ, rather than be forecast (Heb. 2:3–4);

(3) in the entirety of church history following the New Testament era, there has never been anyone who regularly healed people the way Jesus and his apostles did—instantly, completely, repeatedly, and in the hardest cases.

While these arguments do not discount the possibility of modern miracles, they soften our expectation for frequent signs of that type. Many notable theologians held the cessationist view, including John Calvin, Martin Luther, Jonathan Edwards, George Whitefield, Charles Spurgeon, and others.

The case for continuationism is made by the following:

(1) Jesus seems to teach a continuity between his ministry and ours (John 20:21), stretching across enough time for the gospel to be preached to the entire world (Matt. 24:14). Because we did not stop ministering after

Jesus had to stop during his earthly ministry, therefore when he stopped healing on earth, it need not mean we stop doing so in his name;

(2) Jesus says we who believe in him will do the works he did, and even greater things (John 14:12–14);

(3) Acts shares stories of not only statured apostles doing signs but also deacons like Stephen and Philip (6:5–8; 8:6);

(4) Paul teaches that God supplies the miracles by faith, not the law (Gal. 3:5);

(5) Paul teaches about spiritual gifts, not only for apostles but for all believers, including gifts to heal and do miracles (1 Cor. 12:7–10).

So what can we say? By faith we make room for miracles, but we need not make miracles the *only* criterion for sacred guidance. Other supernatural experience comes, either created by God for our particular direction or naturally occurring episodes in which God heightens our awareness to find the stars we're looking for. In stewarding this mystery, sanction your interpretation of your experiences with Scripture, by clear impression in prayer, and by confirmation from the counsel of mature believers.

It Was Bizarre but Beautiful

In 2002, my wife, Tammy, and I tried to steward this mystery. It was a big one—a real, high-stakes gut check. By watching for signs of change across just five months, we sold or stored everything we had and moved to South Korea.

For three years prior to this decision, Tammy prayed, journaled, and felt an impression of mind that—and this is a direct quote—"something bizarre is going to happen." She wasn't fearful but expectant, and began praying that God would reveal it to me. The dates of her journal proved a longevity of what the old-timers call a quickening of the spirit, or anticipation in God. What she didn't know was that I had imagined that bizarre thing too—but we never told each other.

We attended a large church conference in Indianapolis for our denomination, and while walking past the International Higher Education display tables, she pointedly asked, "Have you ever thought about working overseas?" That jolted me.

"Actually," I replied, "I haven't told you something for about a year because I thought you'd think I'm nuts. I've kind of been dreaming about that."

She smiled like she knew something I didn't. We picked up some literature and talked to a guy who told us, to our surprise, that they needed someone of our background immediately in Korea. It was professional whiplash! We had both assumed this new-to-us idea would take many years to come to fruition.

That night we attended a worship service. Guess who sang? The Korean Women's Choir. Then during the offering, I felt an unusually clear impression of mind from Matthew 7:2: "With the measure you use, it will be measured to you." I felt surveilled by God himself, who was watching for my response. That passage is really about being gracious to others, accepting and nonjudgmental. It's not about getting stuff after giving stuff. It had nothing to do with the country of Korea, but it still pried open any restraint, doubt, or questioning in me. I felt almost uncontrollably open-handed, totally generous of spirit.

With no time to talk to Tammy about it, I followed an immediate impulse to put every dollar I had in the offering plate. The amount is important to the story: $202. It was everything I had, an unusually large stash for me due to the fact that we were currently traveling. It was our meal and gas money. I knew my next trip to an ATM would overdraft our account. We lived within our means, but a young family of five demanded every last penny for repairs, clothes, you name it.

After the service we filled out an interest questionnaire then drove home, thinking this transition would be decades ahead. But Korea kept showing up in our lives. I started seeing "made in Korea" clothing labels that I hadn't noticed before. One night, while flipping mindlessly through TV channels, we landed on a documentary about Korea. We met Korean people. We giggled together about the strangeness of this pattern.

Then, probably two months after Indianapolis, we got a call, asking if we were interested in a faculty position at the Korean institution, beginning just five months from now. What?! We had every reason to say no: good community, great friends, privileged employment, and three elementary-age kids who were well settled into formative lives.

Worry struck me on a few fronts. First, I didn't even have enough money to fly *one* of us one way to the other side of the world—let alone *five* of us, plus all we'd need for housing, the kids' homeschooling, and more. Second, our eldest daughter had a debilitating anxiety disorder around crowds. It was bad enough that at school she could not enter the cafeteria, and at church she could not pack into children's church. Was I about to thrust my firstborn into one of the most densely populated countries on earth and ruin her forever? Third, it was a short-term assignment, so how could I ever provide my family with stability upon returning to the States? What should we do? What is God saying? I was unsettled, but Tammy wasn't. Then, like rapid fire, three things happened over a couple weeks.

While sitting on our back patio meditating, praying, and reading, my mind went quickly to Matthew 10:37–39: "Anyone who loves their father or mother more than me is not worthy of me; anyone who loves their son or daughter more than me is not worthy of me. Whoever does not take up their cross and follow me is not worthy of me. Whoever finds their life will lose it, and whoever loses their life for my sake will find it." Wow. It was like God was saying, *You are spooked by this, but there is a fuller life for you on the other side.*

Next, I told Tammy I felt strongly that I should do something I'd never done before: stay awake all night praying and begging God for confirmation. One of the themes in that prayer was confessing my worry about stability for the family. The next morning, on an ordinary Thursday, I entered the copy room of my workplace around ten o'clock when the secretary buzzed on the intercom saying, "A man named Jay Martinson is on the phone for you." I didn't know him, but I took the call. He was a department chair at a Christian university in the States, he had obtained my resumé from a guy I didn't know and couldn't remember sharing it with, and he said my background so perfectly fit a position he had open for three years that if I'd meet to talk, there might be a future. He ended up offering me an open contract, holding a job for me when we felt our Korean service was finished. Wow.

We decided these stars were part of a constellation. God was leading. So we called the folks in Korea and accepted the assignment. But with only about three months before we left, we still had no money to support the family through this adventure. By faith, we proceeded. Faith is simply trusting a promise on the credibility of the Promiser. After writing letters, making phone calls, and speaking in several locations, I was astounded by the result. In just six weeks, we raised $100,000 in pledges, more than enough for our expenses and a substantial sum we could donate to a university we had not yet served!

But here's a miracle amidst the mundane signs. When I looked at the donor roll, guess how many people stood with us. Two hundred and two, exactly. Do you remember the Indianapolis offering? Two hundred and two dollars. "With the measure you use, it will be measured to you."

I'm getting goosebumps all over again as I type this. And by the way, our daughter did just fine with her crowd anxiety over there.

Test this story against how Paul and the Avants stewarded the mystery. Scripture? Check! Clear impression of mind in prayer? Check! Confirmation from mature believers that we interpreted the constellation well? Check! We experienced Type III supernatural awareness for mundane things (Korean choir, clothing labels, documentary, etc.), Type II episodes that may have been created by God for our guidance (an invitation in Indianapolis and from Korea), and even a Type I miracle: 202.

Your Turn

In chapter 1, we explored how new or maturing Christians can be inexperienced or even suspicious of stewarding mysteries of God in the projects or ambitions of our lives. Here in chapter 2, we have examined how the beginning of any ambition is watchfulness for signs of change. If you don't yet know what your ambition should be but feel a stirring into watchfulness, consider these questions from Ruth Haley Barton:

1. What is your response when Jesus asks, "What do you want me to do for you?"

2. Take a step backward. How does a choice you are currently considering fit with others' observations of who you are and what God is doing in your life?

3. Take a step forward. Which choice might you wish you made if you were on your deathbed?

4. Does God bring to mind any scripture that has direct bearing on the decision?

5. Which alternative is the most life-giving (John 10:10), peacemaking (Phil. 4:7), and gives freedom in the Spirit (2 Cor. 3:17)?

6. Which alternative fosters a deeper level of surrender to God and love of one another?[8]

If you already have a project in mind, and can begin discerning remarkable meaning from so-called mundane experiences, read Mark 8, and hear the tone and expectation in Jesus's words. The disciples worry they have no bread on their journey. Jesus asks them pointed questions: "When I broke the five loaves for the five thousand, how many basketfuls of pieces did you pick up?" (v. 19). And of course they answer twelve. "And when I broke the seven loaves for the four thousand, how many basketfuls of pieces did you pick up?" (v. 20). And of course they answer seven. Then Jesus asks, "Do you still not understand?" (v. 21). He is saying, *When you get clear that I am leading you, I will supply your need.*

Look at the artifacts of your life and apply the three principles described in this chapter:

1. How does Scripture sanction what you feel led to do?

2. Do you have a recurring impression of mind in prayer?

3. Do mature believers in your life affirm your interpretation of God's leading?

If the answer to all three questions is yes, then you're on your way. But if you're not sure about the timing, that's another mystery to steward. We examine it in chapter 3.

THREE
WHEN TO START
(THE TIMING OF GOD)

While psychiatrists combat ADD, attention deficit disorder, we should not lose sight of TDD, time deficit disorder. It is even more epidemic.

A few years ago, demolition experts wired the Georgia Dome in Atlanta for implosion, clearing way for a new home for the Atlanta Falcons, the $1.6 billion Mercedes-Benz Stadium. Across the street sat Jason Rudge, a staffer for The Weather Channel, who had been livestreaming for forty minutes and was prepared to film a rare pyrotechnic spectacle. Others gathered too, on the opposite curb, closer to the dome—nearly twenty pedestrians bubbling with anticipation.

What happened next inspired more than a million YouTube views. Faint voices chant on the video a countdown to collapse, "5, 4, 3, 2, 1." On the final syllable, a city bus slides from right to left into the camera view, parking in the direct sight line of the dome.

The cameraman grunts in frustration, "No, bus! Get out of the way, bus!" while July 4th-style detonations crack and smoke billows, eclipsed almost entirely by the bus. Four or five beeps cover the cameraman's expletives. The dome topples. A mushroom cloud of debris arches above the bus, confirming what could not be seen on camera. It's down. He missed it all.

Then, like some sort of *Saturday Night Live* skit, scripted for impossibly humorous timing, the dome exhales a final plume of dust, and only then does the bus slowly pull away.[1] That cameraman for The Weather Channel experienced a case of TDD, time deficit disorder. He was there at the right time, but he was in the wrong place.

Certainly, we all want to find the right time and the right place. In fact, Bill Gross—the founder of IdeaLab, which facilitated the launch of one hundred companies—reported during a 2015 TED Talk the results of his study on why so few startups succeed. All companies were ranked on five key factors: the power of the product or service idea itself, the nature of the leadership team, the business model, the funding, and the timing in the market. You guessed it! The leading variable contributing to success was fortuitous timing. Ranking at the bottom were funding and business model, an irony to many people because products desired by the public attract funding very quickly and sustain a business until the model matures. That was certainly the case with Facebook and Airbnb, as examples.[2]

Some people work excruciatingly hard to be in the right place, but TDD keeps them in wrong timing. A few years ago, five thousand readers of *USA Today* filed their opinion on the hardest thing to do in sports. Ranking number one was hitting a baseball.[3] The margin of error is tiny. Think through it: factors include the batter's hands, hips, vision; environmental factors like wind and sun; the pitch type affecting ball speed, arc, and delivery. Even if contact is made, the physics set a flight trajectory so difficult they'll pay you millions of dollars if you can put it into fair play just three times of ten.

There's a different kind of TDD in romantic relationships. Often it is the wrong place, wrong time. The patchwork of courtship signaling can be so cumbersome and awkward that reality shows now try to reduce the margin of error by bunching up twenty bachelors with one bachelorette (or vice versa), in a feat of voyeuristic chemistry. Even when producers manufacture the right place, the wrong timing garishly gags viewers with strange pickup lines, inappropriately accelerated physical affection, or peacocking testosterone to run off other suitors. Ultimately, yuck: wrong place, wrong time.

Finally, there is one domain where being at the wrong place at the right time paradoxically pays off, and that is with investment decisions. Markets reward investors for escaping the herd for more isolated, greener pastures, catching little-known stock before it soars upward. A *Harvard Business Review* study of pharmaceutical launches shows that "the average firm in the study . . . could increase its market value by $702 million if it reduced the irregularity [timing] of its launches by 10%."[4] If you can excel at this, you might even earn a nickname like Warren Buffett's Oracle of Omaha. Buffett began in 1956 with a $10,000 investor. Today, Berkshire Hathaway wholly owns Dairy Queen, Duracell, Geico, Fruit of the Loom, and large portions of Wells Fargo, Heinz, Coca-Cola, and more.[5] Oracle timing, indeed.

You get it, right? While there is more than just timing going on here, timing is still a significant variable. Whether it's demolition, dating, or home-run dingers, folks all across your city, state, and country are making massively important decisions about when to act, creating glorious—or debilitating—results. Generally, people carry fewer questions about *what* to do but gigantic ones about *when* to do it. Households, companies, and even countries hang in the balance. In the wisdom of Homer, don't become wise too late.

But in the wisdom of God, we hold an ancient, resilient hope of a Spirit-guided life, marked by optimal timing, on matters important to God. In this lives a mystery that matters about the timing of God: he delays then directs; permits ambiguity and frustration, followed by conviction with confirmation. In the God moment, we feel in our spirit, now! Now is the time!

Delay with Direction for Paul—and Even Jesus

The apostle Paul struggles to steward this mystery, as do we. In some episodes, his confidence and clarity to discern timing guidance abound. In others, Paul knows the frustration of ambiguity. We all yearn in our spirit like Habakkuk: "LORD, I have heard of your fame; I stand in awe of your deeds, LORD. Repeat them in our day, in our time make them known; in wrath remember mercy" (3:2). A pit grows in our stomachs as we wonder, *When, God?!*

First, look at Paul's confidence in 2 Corinthians: "We [relied] not on worldly wisdom but on God's grace. . . . Because I was confident of this, I wanted to visit you first so that you might benefit twice. I wanted to visit you on my way to Macedonia and to come back to you from Macedonia, and then to have you send me on my way to Judea. Was I fickle when I intended to do this? Or do I make my plans in a worldly manner so that in the same breath I say both 'Yes, yes' and 'No, no'? . . . I call God as my witness—and I stake my life on it—that it was in order to spare you that I did not return to Corinth" (1:12c, 15–17, 23).

Second, however, Paul's Godward gaze suspends in uncertainty. After two years in Ephesus, he feels "compelled by the Spirit" to move to Jerusalem (see Acts 20:22; see also 19:10, 21). Turbulence along the way does not dissuade him—not a two-hour riot (19:23–41); nor the scare of a dead man later healed (20:7–12); not even his sorrow at relational separation (20:36–38). In fact, Paul is "in a hurry to reach Jerusalem" (20:16). Yet how strange when, at one stop toward Jerusalem, arriving at Tyre, Paul finds himself delayed: "Through the Spirit they urged Paul not to go on to Jerusalem" (21:4b). Imagine Paul's confusion when, at the same time he is feeling compelled to go, his confidantes say, *We think God wants you to stay put!*

In Acts 16, another curious misdirection must put Paul's head on a swivel. He is the Billy Graham of his time, and can fill synagogues or stadiums without much advertising. Yet, twice, his ministry intentions are blocked by God. He and his team "traveled throughout the region of Phrygia and Galatia, having been kept by the Holy Spirit from preaching the word in the province of Asia. When they came to the border of Mysia, they tried to enter Bithynia, but the Spirit of Jesus would not allow them to" (vv. 6–7). Eventually, God gives Paul a vision during the night, and everyone concludes it means it is time for Paul to head to Macedonia (vv. 9–10). This episode demonstrates an irony of Christian life: even a God*ward* agenda—one of zealous, authentic intent to please God—might not be *God's* agenda. For example, Paul previously used his pre-conversion identity as a defender of the Jewish faith—on behalf of God—to justify his persecution of the followers of Jesus (see Acts 9:1–2).

A different series of episodes—less dramatic but still clear—illustrate how Paul wants to act before God does. Paul becomes aware that Rome is a revival land, a Christian hotspot reported all over the world, yet he has been assigned elsewhere: "I do not want you to be unaware, brothers and sisters, that I planned many times to come to you (but have been prevented from doing so until now) in order that I might have a harvest among you, just as I have had among the other Gentiles" (Rom. 1:13; see also vv. 8–12). He is "eager" (v. 15) but has to wait. In Corinth, new converts suffer under power dynamics of leaders in the region. Paul says, "But I will come to you very soon, if the Lord is willing" (1 Cor. 4:19a). Later, he wishes to spend the winter with them (16:5–6) but only "if the Lord permits" (v. 7).

Now get this one. Even Jesus, perfectly attuned to the Holy Spirit, throws a curveball to his disciples in what appears to be duplicity: saying one thing and doing another. In John 7, he stays in Galilee to avoid a scheme by Jewish leaders in Judea to kill him. But when the Jewish Festival of Tabernacles arrives, his brothers urge him to attend this weeklong event commemorating God's provision of manna in the desert: "Leave Galilee and go to Judea, so that your disciples there may see the works you do. No one who wants to become a public figure acts in secret. Since you are doing these things, show yourself to the world" (vv. 3–4).

Curiously, Jesus replies, "You go to the festival. I am not going up to this festival, because my time has not yet fully come" (v. 8).

Then, after they leave, he secretly goes to the festival anyway (see v. 10). Huh?

Timing: Learn to Discern

Did Jesus lie?! As the incarnate God, lying is not something Jesus ever did (see Num. 23:19; Titus 1:2; Heb. 6:18). But Jesus also does not bow to the will of his brothers. He obeys only God's will. The same should be true for us; we must steward a mystery that matters. When we learn to discern— once we have a vocabulary of timing—we are better equipped to understand what God is doing and when.

Stuart Albert, a visiting professor to Harvard and MIT, is also a timing expert who consults for companies of all sizes on strategic timing issues. He says we wrongly assume that life is composed of serial moments, doing one thing, then the next, the next, and so on. Actually, we live in a massively parallel world, with a multiplicity of cross-current factors set to differing timing arcs. "Deciding when to act depends on the length of interval [you occupy]. If time is limited and a lengthy task can't be shortened, it's foolish to begin. It would be like trying to force an SUV into a parking space barely big enough for a bicycle. In order to plan effectively, we need to be able to estimate how long something will take and how long events or conditions in the environment will last," which is, he says, "the heart of the question of timing. Yet before we can estimate an interval of time, we need to recognize one is present."[6] Timing analysis cannot predict the future, but it can clarify patterns at work that have previously been unexamined. Knowing them equips us to interpret what God might be doing in real time, and fortify our choices in it.

Here is our vocabulary of time. The events of our lives could feature one or several dynamics:

- **Pace**. How fast is an issue in your life moving, like a runner who speeds up or slows down during a race? In the education industry, MOOCs—massive, open, online courses—appeared suddenly as an innovation we all thought might ruin us, but they didn't last.

- **Interval**. How long is a pause likely to last, like a runner who stops to catch their breath? In my institution, we stopped offering a few degrees because the program accreditation requirements were onerous and expensive. We had every intention of adding them back in if the regulations ever changed.

- **Duration**. How long will something continue, like a marathon or sprint? In education, online classes (not MOOCs) were met with skepticism in the late 1990s, but shazam! They're still here, and they're not going away any time soon!

- **Shape**. As an issue develops, how suddenly might it accelerate or decelerate, like a runner who has great stamina for a burst of energy in the final stretch? In the planning work of my institution, we try to remain coiled toward launching a new facility or program but only spring into action when the right lineup of donors appears. I am shocked by how fast something can come together, but it takes enormous patience for that burst.

- **Cycles**. Is there a seasonal factor to consider, like a runner who performs better (or worse) at the end of a long and grueling competition schedule? In education, there are macroeconomic dynamics creating the longest enrollment contraction in seventy-five years, which has little to do with prowess or the skills of people.

It could be one or any combination of these things, like a polyphony—multiple and simultaneous notes in sheet music. Sheet music shows how different instruments sound off at the same time, which can be harmonious or disastrous! Albert says timing experts learn to read the sheet music of our lives not left to right (sequentially) but up and down (concurrently). Is there enough harmony to act now, or would it be better to wait until later?

Albert's research shows that decisions about timing actually feature up to twenty concurrent variables, but most people only identify half that many. His management challenge is the "second dozen exercise"—discipline one's thinking to name more factors that could influence your idea. In track, consider an athlete who didn't sleep well last night, then ate too heavy a breakfast, then is saddened to find that her estranged dad, who promised to attend the meet, is missing from the stands, then endures a spiteful admonishment from her coach, plus the humidity is high, a seam in her running shoe has torn—and if all that weren't enough, she's also distracted by a history test tomorrow, which she can't make time to study for because of an afterschool job.

You see? Learn to discern.

Let's go back to Jesus in John 7. We aren't catching him in a lie about the festival. We need not question Jesus's readiness, courage, clarity, or morality—but we can diagnose his polyphony of timing factors to explain this. The brothers talk in serial time: he has done miracles and grown in popularity, so now he can do more miracles and get even more popular! But his discernment slows his pace. He goes to the festival in secret (v. 10) and waits until the time is right to make himself known (v. 14).

The brothers want him to show off in order to assuage doubt since they are still not sure about Jesus (see vv. 3–5). But he isn't going to pander to them. The brothers have a case of TDD. Instead, Jesus lets the shape of time turn at the festival for teachers to expose their own heresy. This way, he shows up to refute them, rather than becoming a carnival spectacle of miraculous works. Jesus's teaching at the festival gave us a doctrine of the Holy Spirit that lasts to this day (see vv. 37–39).

This is how we steward the mystery of timing guidance. It loosens our preoccupation with substance in our lives—the business plan, the community service staff, the budget—and reveals cross-current influences on our choice to act or wait. This diagnosis cannot predict the future or change God's agenda, but by its knowledge we can coil ourselves, ready to be sprung by God at a moment he creates for us.

Value in Delay: Seven Tests of Timing

God is impeccable. He is never late, rarely early, and does not leave us without meaning during our intervals of silence. Our job is to reflect and watch for his catalyst out of the silence.

First, wait expectantly, not passively. An expectant person is hopeful when the pace slows, anticipating the shaping work of God, but a passive person is impatient and doubtful. Joyce Meyer says, "The passive person has a lot of wishbone but not much backbone!"[7] In a different article on the same topic, she says, "God wants us to live by discernment—revelation knowledge, not head knowledge. . . . When you're willing to say, 'God, I can't figure this out, so I'm going to trust you to give me revelation that will set me free,' then you can be comfortable in spite of not knowing."[8]

Second, don't act impulsively. Cindi McMenamin says that, during our waiting, we are tempted to push open doors God doesn't put in front of us. We should not act if that choice compromises Scripture, such as working so hard we neglect church attendance (Heb. 10:25), joining partnerships that dishonor God (2 Cor. 6:14), or entering into circumstances that present temptations away from intimacy with God—for God does not tempt us to sin (James 1:13–14). Those types of actions signal an acceleration past God's timing.[9]

Third, go deep. Instead of grieving the length of your interval, concentrate on it so that godliness grows. Focus, then expand. In this sense, waiting can be good! James 1:2–4 says, "Consider it pure joy, my brothers and sisters, whenever you face trials of many kinds, because you know that the testing of your faith produces perseverance. Let perseverance finish its work so that you may be mature and complete, not lacking anything." Hebrews 11:6 says, "And without faith it is impossible to please God, because anyone who comes to him must believe that he exists and that he rewards those who earnestly seek him." In this way, God's interest in your interval is more about holiness than health, wisdom than wealth, sanctification than some generic version of success.

Fourth, apply some criteria tests for the readiness of your project or ambition. I suggest seven, a few of which came to me from a deeply experienced executive coach who developed them while consulting Fortune 500 companies; others I created and have tested myself as discernment tools in timing.

I'll tell you a story about this. In the nature of my profession, I am always working on things that take three to five years to come to fruition. As a result, fulfillment runs deep on ribbon-cutting days for programs or facilities that will support students or meet community needs. But in another respect, how vulnerable it is to publicly commit to solving a long-term problem without yet knowing where the ideas, money, or staffing will come from!

In late 2017, we hit a timing cycle. Having concluded a five-year run on several priorities, we paused to surveil the environment again and determine new, large-scale problems to solve. If people have confidence in the process and the criteria for naming priorities, consent and adoption will triumph over mere announcement. Our process is probably similar to other things you already practice or have heard about in strategic-planning vernacular, with one exception: we also do SWOT analyses, looking for our strengths, weaknesses, opportunities, and threats. We scan industry literature, use past performance data, pay for consultants on specialized topics; we listen through focus groups, interviews, and web surveys; and we test our conclusions before committing with feedback from key leaders, advisory panels, trustees, and the like.

But that might bore you with predictability, right? That's not why you picked up this book. Of course, God guides through all sorts of processes like that, but the secret sauce to our due diligence is a spiritual-discernment activity threaded through it. Simply put, we believe—from Scripture, the long tradition of the church, and our own experience—that God guides a group of mature believers who seek him. Such seeking takes different forms. In chapter 1, you heard about our discovery of Rashad from fasting, individual and corporate prayer, and Scripture. We did that in our priority-setting process too. I keep pictures of prayer sessions by our leaders because those memories lend me confidence when things derail.

When you're in a cycle, seeking God's timing, remember what Henry and Richard Blackaby say: there is no lack of aspiring leaders, but "society's great deficit" is *spiritual* leaders. Society doesn't merely need people who get things done. "Adolph Hitler did that. The world needs professionals who know how to apply their faith in the boardroom, in the classroom, in the courtroom, and in the operating room. Jesus summed up this truth for every executive, politician, schoolteacher, lawyer, doctor, minister, and parent when he said: 'But seek first the kingdom of God and his righteousness, and all these things will be provided for you' (Matt. 6:33)."[10] Because discipleship requires estrangement from earthly principles, *spiritual* leaders are necessary to break us free from inconsequential talk. (A financial problem might not be about business strategy but about living outside God's agenda, or harboring private sin, removing favor and blessing.) A spiritual leader's primary job is not to dream up something big for God, tell people, then figure out how to accomplish it. It is to figure out what God blesses, and do that. Spiritual leaders identify God's purposes and align their institutions accordingly.

By late fall 2017, our planning group of fifteen found themselves in a wintry log cabin to decide what all this due diligence meant for us. It was time to decide which options were well timed. As snow dusted the trees outside and our stone fireplace crackled, we posted seven tests of strategy and timing on a wall and sorted the good from the better. (Mind you, at this stage, I still have no idea how we fund or staff any of the proposals, so I deeply rely on the Holy Spirit to move us from ambiguity to conviction.) In the seven tests, we ask about the proposed project:

1. Is it credible to those it intends to benefit? (This is a test against inward preoccupations, and for the perspective of those whom we serve. If not, timing is bad. Action is premature.)

2. Is it realistic to those who must implement it? (This is a test against unfunded mandates to do more with less. If not yet realistic, we have a timing problem again. Wait and perfect.)

3. Is it attractive to overseers and funders? (This test honors the objectivity of advisors, trustees, bankers, donors.)

4. Can it be accomplished in a timeframe of five years? (This tests against both small, sand-bagging ideas that could happen on their own in one year, *and* overreaching plans that would take so long to accomplish the project strategy would become ineffective before the project finished.)

5. Can funding be arranged within our timeline? (This tests our discipline for scale.)

6. Is the level of risk appropriate? (This tests our bias to act on something with only 75 percent of the information we wish we had to decide, rather than delay until all are satisfied with 100 percent.)

7. Does the Holy Spirit give us unity as we spiritually discern God's leading toward these choices? (My notes for the meeting said, "We want something big enough to demand corporate spiritual unity, not mere teamwork. Convictionless support is not our objective, but hearing from God." This test is anchored on Ps. 133, John 14:26, Acts 15:28, and Acts 16:10, as discussed in chapter 2. Unity means we find prevailing support; it does not require a unanimous vote.

We spent all day at it. And guess what? Four priorities met all the tests. We later found prevailing support from five additional groups. The breadth and depth of endorsement were extraordinary. Test #7 is king, making a palpable and infectious dynamic in our work. However, it grieved many of us that a fifth priority didn't pass all the tests. There were timing issues. But three years later, something surprising happened. I'll come back to that.

After Ambiguity, Conviction Comes

A premise in this mystery that matters is that God's delay *is* direction. Just as birthing a premature baby threatens its health, and delaying until full term provides a healthier incubation period, so too are your ambitions under God's timing. Eventually, conviction comes with confirmation. Four of our proposals showed a compelling readiness, but one didn't.

What does conviction feel like? For some, spiritual conviction feels like surging urgency. One of the world's foremost authorities on leadership and change, John Kotter, says that 70 percent of work situations where substantial change is needed fail for lack of urgency. "Urgent behavior is not driven by a belief that all is well or that everything is a mess but, instead, that the world contains great opportunities and great hazards. Even more so, urgent action is not created by feelings of contentment, anxiety, frustration, or anger, but by a gut-level determination to *move . . . now*."[11] Spiritual conviction makes people unusually alert and proactive. But because feelings are more influential than thoughts for producing change, documents hold less power than story. In Christian jargon, call it *testimony*—holding forth on what God has guided you to do, and do now.

For others, spiritual conviction feels like intuition: sudden surety despite detail. As Keener says, Greek philosophy was the context of Paul's writings, and it often equated spiritual revelation with intuition. "As important as reason is, the highest mysteries were available only in direct encounter with God."[12] Similarly, Malcom Gladwell challenges our culture's default in his bestselling book *Blink*, which assumes that the quality of a decision relates to the amount of time and effort put into it—a look-before-you-leap mentality. However, we often know things intuitively, quickly, and reliably. In some cases, "extra information isn't actually an advantage at all; in fact, you need to know very little to find the underlying signature of a complex phenomenon."[13]

This reasoning bears out in research on decision-making. Snap judgments made by teachers, romantic partners, doctors, military leaders, and even improv comedians are surprisingly dependable. Says Gladwell, "We need to respect the fact that it is possible to know without knowing why we know and accept that sometimes we're better off that way."[14] Training in jazz music, for example, produces a learned spontaneity. Musicians learn default rhythms of basic and repeatable structures while making space for freelance riff. Spontaneity isn't random, but cued. It's the same in basketball. Teammate positioning on a fast break or an offense set to triangle is trained, but it allows for a wide range of idiosyncratic decisions. This is a wonderful analogy for what Paul calls our competence in the Spirit (2 Cor. 3:6). As reviewed in chapter 2, there are stable methods to interpret God reliably, yet God's leading often feels personalized. From this comes a form of conviction that feels like intuition, and from it we are compelled to act—now.

For still others, spiritual conviction might feel like ideation and action. Theoretical physicist Leonard Mlodinow writes about how the gene DRD4 as a dopamine receptor drives us to become discontent with the status quo, rewarding us with pleasure when we experience new things. Those with a more active gene experience *neophilia*, a love for novelty and change, while others whose brains produce low levels are *neophobic*, fearing change. In that stimulus for something new in our lives, our brains afford what Mlodinow calls "elastic thinking."[15] Contrasted with analytical thinking to logically diagnose what is known or familiar, elastic thinking is a brain in free association, where ideas or solutions arrive without knowing where they come from. A person senses a new and profound ability to let go of conventional ideas, comfort with ambiguity or contradiction, a new capacity to question, openness to new paradigms, reliance more on imagination than logic, and, among others, willingness to experiment and tolerate failure. It is possible that God builds spiritual conviction through our brain chemistry—after all, he created it!—in ways that convert neophobes into neophiliacs!

Certainly, our spiritual conviction can be wrong! Accountability to Scripture and confirmation from mature believers can correct wrong convictions (see chapter 2). The Nobel Prize-winning economist Daniel Kahneman describes various susceptibilities to trusting one's intuition. One could suffer: *halo effects*, which exaggerate one's sense of infallibility; *anchoring effects*, which shackle a person to their first impressions despite valuable new information; or *narrative effects*, which exclude details that contradict the storyline a person hopes to embody.[16]

Your Turn

In chapter 2, we explored how Paul found remarkable guidance from what can appear to be mundane experiences, Types I, II, or III. In this chapter, we have learned how delay becomes direction and how ambiguity turns toward conviction with confirmation. We have learned a vocabulary of time to discern God's rhythm.

Remember the fifth priority our strategic-planning group had to set aside? Across the seven criteria, the timing was bad for lack of capacity and funding. Well, little did we know that, simultaneous with our planning in the fall of 2017, God inspired an out-of-the-blue professional relationship with someone across the country who taught us the foundations for our idea (capacity), stirred the inspiration of an alumna with financial means to support it (a substantial boost of $350,000), and sent us three fantastic employees to operate it whom we hardly strained to find. Three years later, in the fall of 2020, we launched.

In hindsight, God directed us by delaying us, creating an interval of three years. While we grieved the delay, we later learned a parallel shaping of time was also at work in our polyphony of factors to manage.

Now it's your turn. In the project you steward:

(1) Take the "Second Dozen" Polyphony challenge. Most people can passively name twelve concurrent influences on a decision, but you're becoming an expert! Name twenty. Go ahead, write them down!

(2) Do you experience problems or opportunities with pace, interval, duration, shape, or cycle?

(3) Diagnose the readiness of your project on the seven tests of strategy and timing. How many tests does your idea pass?

I hope you have a little more clarity on whether to wait or go. It might now be time to receive accomplices to your cause. Let's examine that in chapter 4.

FOUR
ACCOMPLICES YOU DIDN'T RECRUIT

I love the African proverb that says, *if you want to go fast, go alone; if you want to go far, go together.* Partners in your cause make all the difference. But how to find them?

Two years ago, Jorge and Raquel approached me in the back of a room. We had just concluded three days with a large group of Hispanic leaders in Houston, coaching one another toward the future. Behind their beaming faces and flashing eyes came a hopeful announcement.

The cadence of Spanish-to-English translation left me a step behind the content of their enthusiasm. "We believe God"—translation—"might be telling us"—translation—"to move from Costa Rica to Indiana"—translation—"to work with you." They giggled, shrugging shoulders, acknowledging the weird spontaneity of the idea.

Obvious complications arose. What about their children? Visas? The language barrier? Besides all that, I didn't have an open position!

But something beyond language passes between folks who follow God. We know that God sometimes does this. So even if, in the moment, we believe Jorge and Raquel's idea is not probable, in God we always affirm it is possible. Then we proceed without suspicion and simply look for confirmation. Rashad navigated this in chapter 1. So did the Avants in chapter 2. We did it in Korea in chapter 3. God directs people to carry a cause together. Many times I have sat slack-jawed, receiving stunningly talented colleagues whose arrival cannot be attributed to human effort—the CFO of the Smithsonian Institution ends up in my Illinois project; the head of recruitment for America's largest Christian university lands in my Indiana project; the director of all North American manufacturing for General Motors helps fund my Korea project. I've come to expect God's fingerprints on talent and timing.

Mark Batterson and Richard Foth write about divine assignments in *A Trip around the Sun.* They reference Paul's words in Ephesians 2:10: "For we are God's handiwork, created in Christ Jesus to do good works, which God prepared in advance for us to do." Batterson and Foth explain that the Ephesian churches to whom Paul writes hear these words in the context of their Middle Eastern culture: when a ruler embarks on a journey, his servants leave a few days earlier, "to prepare the way for the king. They were his secret service, his advance team." But, they say, "the heavenly Father flips this concept for us, his servants. Instead of servants taking care of their king, the King of kings takes care of his servants. The picture painted in this passage is simply this: God is setting you up! He is in the business of strategically positioning us in the right place at the right time. And his angels are our advance team."[1]

Were Jorge and Raquel my advance team for an emerging possibility? I didn't know yet, but we departed Houston with a sense of responsibility to do the chapter 2 stuff—looking for signs of change. Two years have now passed, and I still don't know, but my radar remains alert. Their contact information still rests two feet from me, on a credenza, waiting.

If you need collaborators for a project, here is a mystery that matters: God often sends accomplices we don't recruit, and they become "Godsends" in every sense of the word as they discover their calling and gifts that complement our own.

God's Human Resources Department around Paul

Packed densely around Paul are purposeful and timely associates, all following God's lead. Half of the thirteen epistles attributed to Paul conclude with a directory of names, nearly eighty people listed in all—accomplices to his cause. Sometimes, there were thirty names (Rom. 16), other times fifteen (2 Tim. 4), and in Ephesians 6 Paul's benediction boils down to a singular mention, Tychicus, who is sent "that he may encourage you" (v. 22). Paul understands the notion: sent, not recruited. Ananias encounters Paul specifically for his conversion (Acts 9:10–19). When hardship comes, God sends Titus to comfort him (2 Cor. 7:6).

In 1 Corinthians 16, we find Paul leading, planning, giving directions on finances, then moving into team arrangements. He will endorse people they assign (v. 3), then reflect on human resources for different tasks. Timothy must need a compassionate assignment: "See to it that he has nothing to fear while he is with you" (v. 10). In contrast, Apollos must be an independent thinker, equipped for a tough crowd: "I strongly urged him to go to you with the brothers. He was quite unwilling to go now, but he will go when he has opportunity" (v. 12). Don't forget emissaries of encouragement: "Stephanas, Fortunatus, and Achaicus . . . refreshed my spirit and yours also. Such men deserve recognition" (vv. 17a, 18).

New Testament scholar Felix Just has categorized a comprehensive personnel network huddled around Paul, comprising folks with different gifts and roles. There are his *koinonoi* ("equal partners"), whom he did not convert yet who work alongside him for the same cause; his *tekna* ("spiritual children"), whom he converts and toward whom he has pastoral instincts; and his *synergoi* ("fellow worker"), whom he manages and mentors. Let's look at some specific examples.

Gamaliel is Paul's teacher, a Jewish rabbi who trained Paul in Jerusalem (Acts 22:3). He could be the same Gamaliel (or his son) who defends the early disciples in Jerusalem (Acts 5:34), although he is probably not a Christian himself.

Gaius is a travel buddy, a Christian from Macedonia who is with Paul in Ephesus (Acts 19:29; 20:4), who hosts Paul and the church in Corinth (Rom. 16:23); and who is one of the few people Paul has personally baptized (I Cor 1:14). This is probably *not* the same Gaius who is a leader of a Johannine church (3 John 1:1).

Mnason is a caretaker, a Christian from Cyprus who provides Paul and companions hospitality on their journey to Jerusalem (Acts 21:16).

Onesiphorus is a financial donor. Paul sends greetings to his household in Ephesus (II Tim 1:16; 4:19).

Tertius is Paul's secretary, who inserts himself into Paul's letter to the Roman church with his own greeting to that audience: "I, Tertius, who wrote down this letter, greet you in the Lord" (Rom. 16:22).

Apollos is another steward of mysteries (1 Cor. 3:21–4:1), an Alexandrian Jew who has become a Christian missionary and whom Paul describes as eloquent and well versed in Scripture. He preaches and interacts with some of Paul's associates in Ephesus (Acts 18:24–26), in Corinth (Acts 18:27–28), and possibly on Crete (Tit. 3:13).[2]

Following God is demanding and can therefore become lonely. Not everyone is up for it. In fact, Paul was martyred. Honestly, how many of us think we're signing up for that in our discipleship? But imagine his peace, sitting in a jail cell, reminiscing over the people God sent to equip his call. Faces, no doubt, flashed in his memory—a teacher, caretaker, donor, companion, administrative aide, an encourager, a strong-willed one, another steward of mysteries. Frankly, it's amazing. Take a look around your life, and be astonished too. Perhaps God has already sent folks you need—or is in the middle of that process right now.

Calling

One way to steward the mystery that God provides accomplices you don't recruit is to query their calling to see how it complements your own. People are not made for everything, but every single one of us is made for something. You didn't cook this up; God put it in you. A calling is bigger than merely what you like to do, or what others affirm in you—it is what God created you to do. The set of tasks you call your "job" are too small an ambition. Even decades of stitched-together jobs we call a "career" can lack impact or fulfillment. Even when our success justifies toiling labor, if our work lacks a Godward agenda, it may fail to satisfy.

This calling from God echoes through many scriptures: God sets the exact time and place of all people, that we might seek and find him, though he is not far from us (Acts 17:26); God prepared in advance good works for us to do (Eph. 2:10); God tells us to press on and take hold of that for which Christ took hold of us (Phil. 3:12); Paul constantly prays for fellow believers, that God might count them worthy of the calling and that, by God's power, fulfill every good purpose and every good act prompted by their faith (2 Thess. 1:11). But beware—following God's call isn't all roses, which we take up in chapter 8.

We can contrast calling with careerism. A careerist asks herself, "Is this good for me?" or, "Will it improve my standard of living?" or, "Will it provide a launching pad for a next thing?" or, "Does it enhance my resumé or reputation?" But one in pursuit of a calling goes deeper than, "What is my desire?" and gets more precisely into, "What did God create me to do, and am I serving that?" This shift changes everything. Once we abide in our calling, we find meaning and endurance despite difficulty.

Let me walk you through a narrative that is common to Christians. Perhaps you rediscover yourself in this journey of spiritual formation. One day, a faith in God awakened you. You didn't manufacture your faith. It arrived. God made the first move, revealing himself to you. Then you did what only some do—you responded. Faith is believing a promise on the credibility of the Promiser. Just as you put faith in the credentials and sincerity of a bridge engineer to cross a roadway over a hundred-foot cavern, or put faith in the training and accuracy of a pharmacist to allocate life-saving drugs, religious faith means the Scripture I read and Spirit I sense and body of Christ I observe are a credible guide for my soul. You put your faith in Jesus to forgive sin, remove shame and distance from God, and trust that, because he arose, you can too in full peace with God, all forgiven. You had a sense that God drew close to guide you. To accomplish that, he put his Spirit in you. Wow, did things change! Scripture came alive. You began hungering for what pleased God, you enjoyed being with God's people, and the salty things of the world lost their appeal. An inner angst and nagging conscience melted away. Peace and purpose rose. Over the years, you matured, became self-aware, more articulate of your inner life, and slowly came to know, from that invisible place where convictions grow, that you are meant for something that fulfills you and is valuable to others.

Os Guinness says in *The Call* that our primary calling is to follow Christ as believers but that a secondary calling is expressed throughout the church in the plural—our various and individual callings.[3] We should not separate religious convictions from occupations because authentic faith cannot ultimately be sequestered or privatized. The way of discipleship is totality—withholding nothing from God, including our work choices. Mere jobs are too small for people, as an exchange of labor for wages. One's calling is deeper, more motivating, and enduring precisely because it is in response to the Caller—God. It's never a question of whether we do our work with an audience in mind (whether boss, spouse, friends, colleagues, clients)—instead, in this case we decide to please an audience of One.

Your calling is near when you discover that:

- There is one *thing* for which you wish to be responsible.
- Duties are meaningful regardless of others' perceptions of success.
- There is wonder in even commonplace things.
- You don't become what you do but do what you are.
- While seeking it, you also feel sought by it.
- It feels more like an aspiration than an obligation.
- It is aimed at public good, not private gain.
- Your desire becomes humble service to God rather than to set yourself apart as special.
- Clarity on calling becomes an antidote to slothfulness for your lost ambition.

Part of this experience is feeling constituted for an assignment (experience, knowledge, talent), constrained to do it (inner motivation), and requiring courage to do it (God leads us to things beyond ourselves, making the results supernatural).

In my personal experience, and from watching others in their experience with calling, eventually your calling becomes a project that you sense God is entrusting to you. You get a keen sense of being assigned to a timely, strategic, necessary role, usually executed through an organization or community you already occupy. This means you should spend only a little time asking your project team, "What's your dream?" and instead ask, "What might be

God's dream for you? For us?" You could think of God's dream for you—your full potential under his equipping—as your calling.

Even court judges understand the gravity and sacredness of calling. I heard an NPR report a few years ago that illustrates this well. An expert Canadian clarinetist, Eric Abramovitz, received national attention as a teenager for his advanced musical talent, and applied for a prestigious conservatory program in Los Angeles to study under a famous clarinet teacher. He was awarded that opportunity—but he didn't know it.

He saw an email in his inbox from the clarinet teacher under whom he had hoped to study, explaining that his application had been rejected. Abramovitz said it was heartbreaking and confusing because he had been confident he was good enough for one of the two open spots. Abramovitz's girlfriend at the time, Jennifer Lee, consoled him, just as we might hope a loved one would do. He passed through dark days and then recovered the courage to apply for a lesser award with a different program where he would have reduced access to the same famous clarinet teacher. During auditions, the clarinet teacher asked him, "Why did you reject the other offer?"

Abramovitz, confused, asked in return, "Why did *you* reject *me*?" Eventually, Abramovitz was able to show the clarinet teacher the rejection email he had received, which the clarinet teacher firmly asserted had not come from him. Abramovitz launched an amateur investigation that revealed the truth: he shared a computer with his girlfriend, who hadn't wanted him to move from Canada to California. She had intercepted Abramovitz's original acceptance email, responded with a declination in his name, and deleted the email before he saw it. Then she manufactured the fake email address to send him the rejection letter.

He broke up with her and then sued her. A Canadian court awarded him 300,000 Canadian dollars in damages for loss of career opportunity, with the judge adding 50,000 dollars in punitive damages for what he called "morally reprehensible conduct," and "the incompensable personal loss suffered by Mr. Abramovitz by having a closely held personal dream snatched from him by a person he trusted." Today, Eric is a principal clarinetist with the Toronto Symphony (and has a new girlfriend).[4]

What does this story have to do with calling? The judge stacked punitive damages on top of his court ruling for a particular reason: it is "morally reprehensible" to suppress the dream of another. Why? It is too precious, too fragile, too valuable to be toyed with like that. But in God, we happily surrender our personal dreams to his dream for us. As Paul writes in Ephesians 4:1, "As a prisoner for the Lord, then, I urge you to live a life worthy of the calling you have received." Any seeker of their calling will find that calling to be durable through life's setbacks.

This orientation converts your project team into a midwifing environment, where we aid others in bringing into reality what God began in them long ago. Your team becomes a conspiracy of good, locating one another's Godward ability. Yes, your project really can be invested with that big purpose.

Spiritual Gifts

Another way to discern whether God sent accomplices you didn't recruit is to query their spiritual gifts. The apostle Paul outlines a variety of spiritual gifts, which are God-given abilities specifically for service to the church. Even if your project team has no explicit Christian purpose, spiritual gifts are still relevant if your coworkers (paid or volunteer) are believers in service to one another.

The Holy Spirit provides supernatural abilities when our souls are saved (1 Cor. 12:7). No one has all the gifts outlined in Scripture, and no single gift goes to everyone (1 Cor. 7:7; 12:29–30), but people often demonstrate more than one. Various scholars count nineteen explicitly identified gifts in Scripture, primarily from Romans 12, 1 Corinthians 12, and Ephesians 4. The premise is that Jesus gave himself up not only for our sins but also to build his church, the bride of Christ (Eph. 5:25). Some people want their salvation without the church. They see imperfections or hypocrisy and sneer at the church without any sense of obligation. They may watch a televangelist and do their own Bible reading—but you can't have a groom without a bride. We are not born into the faith for isolation but for community. In God's church lurk supernatural abilities and synergy for the common good (1 Cor. 12:5–7).

The practice of these gifts enables us to "reach unity in the faith and in the knowledge of the Son of God and become mature, attaining to the whole measure of the fullness of Christ" (Eph. 4:13). These gifts are not status symbols, "for just as each of us has one body with many members, and these members do not all have the same function, so in Christ we, though many, form one body, and each member belongs to all the others. We have different gifts, according to the grace given to each of us" (Rom. 12:4-6a).

Spiritual gifts can be distinguished from personal aptitude or cultivated talents, which are discovered naturally. Examples could include athleticism, artistic genius, scientific acumen, extroversion, and the like. Spiritual gifts, however, are discovered through the study of Scripture and in the practice of ministry. They are not character qualities that all Christians possess; the fruit of the Spirit is what all believers *are* (Gal. 5:22–23), but spiritual gifts depict what individual believers *do*. Usually, people experience intuition in the domain of their spiritual gift: teachers just know when kids aren't learning; mercy givers can detect one in a crowded room who is hurting; leaders automatically anticipate future needs; and so on.

When trying to identify one's spiritual gifts, Kenneth Berding cautions us toward a one-step process instead of two. Instead of asking ourselves first, "What is my gift?" and then, "Where should I serve?", we should simply ask ourselves, "Where should I serve?" Then, as we practice a ministry role or assignment, we discover an endowment from God for it. By contrast, the two-step process can be more preoccupied with locating the gift than actually practicing ministry to others. In that way, a person first takes a spiritual gift assessment, wrestles over its accuracy, then decides later to serve. Berding says that, of the sixteen times Paul uses the term "charisma"—which we translate as "gift" in English—ten of the uses clearly don't, or are unlikely to, refer to special abilities imbued to us. Also, because Paul's writing style makes frequent uses of lists (virtues, vices, qualifications), it may be that the spiritual gifts named in Scripture are only meant to be illustrative and not exhaustive.[5] Ultimately, we should not agonize over trying to figure out which spiritual gift we have, nor should we withhold from serving in ministry because an assessment tool did not confirm we have a particular gift.

Instead, we should occupy ourselves with serving first and foremost. As we minister, we can anticipate the blessing of God to equip us.

Whether the list of spiritual gifts named by Paul is illustrative or comprehensive, our awareness of them is still an important part of self-discovery. It will also help us build language to share among colleagues in a common cause. Jeff Carver, for example, has authored resources, online courses, and a spiritual gifts inventory that has been used by 1.5 million people through his website, spiritualgiftstest.com. The gifts are understood this way:

- Administration comes from the Greek word *kubernesis*, meaning "one who governs." The Holy Spirit enables this Christian to organize and implement plans that might come from others or from their own vision. They make the trains run on time.

- Apostleship comes from the Greek *apostolos*, meaning "one sent with orders." God gifts these people to launch new ministries, take the gospel to new places, reach across cultural boundaries, and develop leaders for this cause. They are sent with authority, as ambassadors.

- Discernment comes from the Greek word *diakrisis*, which is to be able to judge or appraise a person or situation, knowing good from evil. They are perceptive.

- Evangelism comes from the Greek word *euaggelistes*, or "one who brings good news." All Christians support the commission to disciple others in the faith, but some are imbued with special burden for and effectiveness in converting new believers into the faith (Matt. 28:19-20).

- Exhortation, or encouragement, comes from the Greek *parakaleo*, "to strengthen others." This person has unusual capacity to sustain those who waiver in the faith, encourage, or rebuke if necessary to foster spiritual maturity. They are life-giving relaters.

- Faith as a spiritual gift cannot be confused with the saving faith required for all (Eph. 2:8–9). The Greek word for faith, *pistis*, means "unusual confidence or certainty." Those who have the spiritual gift of faith live boldly and model for others unwavering faith in the midst of challenge.

- Giving comes from the Greek word *metadidomi*, which means "to give," and in some places it appears alongside the word *haplotes*, which means "to give with generosity, without pretense." A person with this gift takes special care in locating and meeting needs. They are typically excellent stewards of wealth who live simply in order to care for others.

- Healing comes from the Greek word *iamaton*, which means "healing." There is no guarantee that a person with this gift will be a conduit of God's power to heal someone, since healing is always subject to God's will. But this person carries unusually deep compassion toward the sick, deep trust in God's provision, and is undeterred by delay.

- Interpretation comes from the Greek *hermeneia*, meaning "to explain a message not broadly understood." God reveals the meaning, and they interpret. This gift only operates to edify the church and glorify God with encouragement and blessing (1 Cor. 14:3). It is *not* for speaking on behalf of God to condemn others.

- Knowledge, or word of knowledge, comes from the Greek *gnosis*, meaning "to provide understanding." A person with this spiritual gift recalls Scripture well and applies it effectively.

- Leadership comes from the Greek word *proistemi*, meaning "to protect others." This gift is more people-oriented than task-oriented, more conceptual or visionary than detail-oriented, thus distinguished from the administration gift.

- Mercy comes from the Greek word *eleeo*, meaning "patient and compassionate toward the afflicted." A person with this gift discerns quickly if someone is not doing well, and walks beside them until the burden is lifted.

- The gift of miracles comes from the Greek phrase *energemata dynameon*, meaning "workings of powers." In an earlier chapter, we reviewed the difference between continuationism and cessationism in order to qualify our understanding of this domain, but the plural "powers" likely means that these gifts are diverse. However, the gift is not constant. It is bestowed for particular circumstances and, like healing, is subject to divine will. A person with this gift has a heightened sensitivity to the presence of God.

- Pastor/Shepherd comes from the Greek word *poimen*, meaning "caretaker" or "guardian." They rescue, care for, and nurture people into the faith, often spending large amounts of time with people.

- Prophecy comes from the Greek *propheteia*, or the ability to receive and deliver a divine message. Paul says this gift should be especially desired (1 Cor. 14:1). A person with this gift today differs from Old Testament prophets who spoke authoritatively to record Scripture, often in a "thus says the Lord" style. Scripture is complete (Rev. 22:18). Today, prophets proclaim existing Scripture, rather than creating new truth, with unusually powerful application to people and events. This may take the form of exhortation, correction, inspiration, or other revelations that equip and edify the church.

- Service comes from the Greek *diakonia*, "to wait tables," often translated in the Bible as "ministry," or *antilepsis*, "helping." A person with this gift is unusually inspired to support the community, filling gaps and freeing up others to use their gifts as they should. They tend to be content in the background.

- Teaching comes from the Greek *didaskalos*. We recognize this root in our English word "didactic," which means "to instruct, instill doctrine, explain, expound." James 3:1 warns, "Not many of you should become teachers, my fellow believers, because you know that we who teach will be judged more strictly." A person with this gift loves to study, share insight, and see others apply it. Without this person, the church is vulnerable to error or sin.

- Tongues, from the Greek *glossa* or *glossolalia*, means "to speak in tongues" as an utterance of prayer that glorifies God. Tongues are spoken to God, not people, and can be human languages or unknown ones (Acts 2:1-12; 1 Cor. 14:2). This gift is not a sign of salvation (1 Cor. 12:30), as some contend. Should one speak an unknown tongue in praise of God, it is not to be distracting but orderly and matched to one gifted with interpretation (1 Cor. 14:27–28).

- Wisdom, or uttering wisdom, is from the Greek *sophia* and refers to a person's intimate understanding of righteousness for a decision or situation. They see through confusion and give direction that helps a person or group honor God. James 3:17 says, "But the wisdom that comes from heaven is first of all pure; then peace-loving, considerate, submissive, full of mercy and good fruit, impartial and sincere."[6]

Let me guess: you found yourself in that list. You are beginning to discover that something good and distinguishing lives within you that you didn't cultivate. Now, if God sends you accomplices you didn't recruit, they will very likely possess a spiritual gift that is complementary to yours and others already on your team. Your project team is a Christian community, equipped by God with unusual prowess. Are you in need of wisdom, shepherding, leadership, or discernment? It might be in a cubicle just down the hall or on the other side of your email.

Transparent Teamwork

Indeed, Christian faith is designed for community, not isolation. So is your project. No matter how much research or planning you did, all launches begin in naïveté and eventually face a reality that may not meet expectations. Leaders must make friends with that inevitability and leverage it for the good of their team. Ed Catmull explains from his experience as CEO of both Pixar and Disney Animation that people who take on complicated projects always get lost in the middle, no matter how talented or organized or clear-visioned the leader. The work that groups attempt is often like "a triple back flip into a gale-force wind, and while you're mad for not sticking the landing, it's amazing you're even alive!" But when experimentation is believed to be necessary, and failure with it, we can still enjoy our work with others even as it confounds us. Catmull also says, "If leaders can talk about our mistakes, we make it safe for others, which is why I make a point of being open about our meltdowns. They teach us something—to loosen the grip of fear on us, and to think of the cost of failure as an investment in our future."[7]

It's little wonder that George Barna reminds us, "Jesus's intent was not to raise up eleven future hotshots whose stellar performances would wow the world, but rather to prepare a humble group whose limitations would force them to work together to complete the assignment he gave them. Jesus was training *teams* of leaders, not potential members of the Future CEO Club."[8]

Sarah Miller Caldicott describes a mandate for transparent teams in her book about the success of Thomas Edison. Despite his reputation as a solo inventor, she discovered that the real secret to his success was creating the world's first research and development firm built on the collaboration of small teams. We should take his cue because we are in the midst of a true global reset that will be permanent, mandating organizations to innovate collaboratively "rather than more lumbering annual planning cycles that are too slow. . . . We must reduce dependence on what a lone VP sanctions," she says, "and collaborate around what a team can devise."[9]

Larry Garatoni knows this reality well. As an eighty-two-year-old serial entrepreneur and multimillionaire, owning concurrent businesses from software to assisted care and charter schools, he is long retired and in a mentorship phase. I am his beneficiary. His financial wealth is cloaked behind the humility of Christian faith and a dependence on quality teams. I asked him to name five keys to his unusual success. Laughing, he summarized: "Numbers 1, 2, and 3 are people, people, people!" Even the one time his Minneapolis-based company decayed he said, "It was because I hired wrong."

Brene Brown advises from her research in leadership vulnerability that we create a team culture of transparency, especially during risky phase of a project launch. "If you want a culture of creativity and innovation, start by developing the ability of managers to cultivate an openness to vulnerability in their teams. This, paradoxically perhaps, requires first that they are vulnerable themselves."[10] Vulnerability is necessary for success because "every time someone holds back on a new idea, fails to give their manager much-needed feedback, and is afraid to speak up in front of a client, you can be sure shame played a part. That deep fear we all have of being wrong, of being belittled and of feeling less than, is what stops us from taking the very risks required to move our companies forward."[11] So coach your team this way: "We believe growth and learning are uncomfortable, so it's going to happen here—you're going to feel that way. You're not alone and we ask that you stay open and lean into it."[12] Unfortunately, few people are willing.

It's difficult to propose an idea that might fail. It's risky to challenge the status quo or resist the urge to settle. But Brown says, "When you identify the discomfort, you've found the place where a leader is needed. If you're not uncomfortable in your work as a leader, it's almost certain you're not reaching your potential as a leader."[13]

So do the work of spiritual discernment—during the project, together, being transparent about what you can't yet see clearly and remaining open to the insights of accomplices. Ruth Haley Barton provides excellent counsel in *Pursuing God's Will Together*, saying that every Christian is called to discernment (Rom. 12:2), that it is a mark of Christian maturity (1 John 4:1), and that, ultimately, unity is the fundamental marker of corporate discernment. "Most of us in leadership . . . have a natural bent toward strategic thinking and planning. But every time we have made decisions purely from the standpoint of what is strategic rather than entering first into a process of discernment, we have gotten ahead of ourselves and made mistakes. Just because something is strategic does not necessarily mean it is God's will for us right now. . . . We are not opposed to planning; in fact, it is an important second step. But we are committed to discernment—listening deeply for God's direction—as the precursor to any plans we make."[14]

It's little wonder Paul writes in Acts 15 about the elders having the consent of the whole church (v. 22), about following the leading of the Holy Spirit (v. 28), and about everyone's resultant joy (v. 31).

Your Turn

You know you live an authentic, self-aware life when people spend just ten minutes with you and can perceive your calling and gifting. Finding clarity about that in others is how you steward the mystery that God sends accomplices you never recruited. Now it's your turn.

First, let's borrow Os Guiness's prompts for identifying your calling and that of others, and I'll add a few items. Follow these steps:

- Does a Bible character, Bible story, or Scripture passage resonate more deeply than others? Some call this a "life verse" that reflects your highest aspiration for life.

- Which activities are most meaningful to you, regardless of notoriety or success?
- In what work do you find fruitfulness, fulfillment, and positive feedback from the body of Christ?
- In what way do you get a sense that, while seeking God, God also seeks you?
- What activity feels more like aspiration than obligation, despite how challenging it may be?
- Is there something for which you wish to be responsible, even though others you respect don't care about it as deeply as you?
- What work feels like a stretch and requires courage to do it, even while some part of you feels equipped for it?
- Is this domain of work aimed at public good more than private gain?
- Finish this prompt. It may include a list of activities, not just one: When I am doing _____, that might be my calling!

Second, take the spiritual gifts inventory at Jeff Carver's website, spiritualgiftstest.com, to increase your knowledge of yourself and of your team members. Note that the spiritual gifts of tongues, interpretation of tongues, miracles, and healing are not tested in his inventory because they are self-evident when practiced.

- Which top three spiritual gifts appear to be most likely yours?
- Seek feedback from others who know you well. Do they confirm these results?
- For a full week, assign yourself the task of actively scanning for opportunities to serve others with the gifts, then ask yourself whether doing so improved circumstances for others. What is becoming clearer to you?

Third, read, meditate, and find something to pray about from the Scriptures mentioned in the Rashad story. Appeal to God to send you accomplices you don't recruit.

- In Exodus 35, God summons Bezalel and Oholiab to particular jobs for which they are unusually gifted.

- In 1 Kings 19, Elijah hears from God in a whisper, the content of which becomes his Human Resources mission. Elijah leaves God to anoint kings and a prophet.
- In Genesis 24, a servant of Abraham looks for a wife for his son Isaac and discovers her before he has even finished praying.

Perhaps you now have a clearer idea about your calling and spiritual gifts, and how to identify them in others. Where they complement each other, it may well be that God sent people you didn't recruit for your project, and you can affirm they are Godsends.

Now, whether you've begun on a shoestring budget or are several months in and have hit a brick wall of financial realities, money pressures on your project can certainly rob joy and crush dreams—or they can become a landscape of God's wonders in provision. There is a mystery to steward about that. Let's get into it in chapter 5.

FIVE
GOD REWARDS
FINANCIAL INTEGRITY

Money is a wonderful servant but a terrible master. Leaders often teeter on that principle between investing money from studied risk or collecting more ulcers than profits by being overextended. Other times, a financial surprise strikes under no fault of one's own.

Several years ago I faced the highest-stakes financial dilemma of my life: I had two big, unnerving surprises that were later compounded by a third and fourth disaster.

Here's what went down: within the first couple weeks of a new job, I discovered that revenue projections weren't going to be realized, creating a $1M shortfall with inadequate cash reserves to absorb it. So my first public action was layoffs. Not fun! Two months later, I learned that a twenty-year employee had made errors of serious financial consequence for a second year in a row. After looking into it, I found that his reputation for operating reclusively left folks in his department lacking confidence in the actual status of things. So I supported the divisional VP in terminating his employment. We don't advertise why people get fired, so I again faced criticism.

But these incidents were mere shockwaves. An earthquake was stirring. With the exiting employee cleared from the office, I assigned a forensic team to figure out what was going on. Then came our third trial. Two VPs sat me down in the conference room and closed the door. "We have some serious news," they said with ashen faces. Though our auditors had never cited a problem, the fired employee's procedural errors over several years amounted to a $3.5M reimbursement liability to the federal government.

My eyes flashed. I just sat with it for a moment. After I asked some clarifying questions, they then asked me, "So what do you want to do?" One option was nothing. Nobody knew about it. Our cashless layoff scenario could stabilize faster if we tucked this news under the rug. But we three, behind that closed door, knew that was wrong.

I said, "I don't know how we survive this, but God sees us, and our actions affect his."

We initially told only a few people—employees whose role required the untangling, our board, bankers, auditors, and the government. Secrecy and privacy are different motivations. We didn't actively prevent people from knowing but felt it was unwise to initiate broad disclosure before we understood it. There are at least three types of uncertainty to manage in life, and we felt all of them in this situation: status uncertainty (Are we sure that $3.5M is it? No! It cost us another $500,000 to satisfy secondary and tertiary consequences.); effect uncertainty (Where will the collateral damage go? More layoffs, or worse?); and response uncertainty (the range of options is debatable).

As we discreetly sorted out the mess, palace intrigue simmered. It was like we lived inside a movie script. Faceless G-men in black trench coats visited our business office without warning, to gather files. Calls came in from clients asking why the IRS had asked to verify their tax records associated with our work. Employees who felt the budgetary whiplash from large, fast cuts wanted answers. Eventually, as we brought order to the chaos, we informed our workforce with a fifty-slide PowerPoint of detail.

Then came the fourth problem. Because the liability had to be booked as a non-cash debt on our financial statements—as if we'd taken out a loan of that size—the domino effect tanked our overall financial ratios, obligating the Feds to classify us as "in distress" and require a letter of credit with cash-monitoring status. We had thirty days to find a million dollars and put it in escrow until the matter could be reconciled, and two years to lift our ratios above a formulaic threshold—or face stiffer consequences. We called our bank for the cash, but even though they would collect fifty thousand dollars in interest each year until this fiasco ended, they refused. It is difficult to communicate what it feels like to need a million dollars by Friday. Tick-tock ran the clock. The CFO and I both worked phones from his office most of the day. We secured signatures for the funds a mere twenty-four hours before the deadline.

Meanwhile, we still had to operate, not only in routine projects and managing normal curveballs but also in making decisions on calls for our generosity. Would we host and fund a dinner for pastors and spouses? Yes. Would we provide a semester's tuition for two students whose missionary parents had lost their home from a hurricane in the Caribbean? Yes. After a hundred-year flood in our city that wiped out the business and home of a family attached to our institution, would we waive rental income from one of our properties and let them stay for free? Yes. In doing these things, we barely lived within our means, but we gave to others despite our massive loss, trusting that God would rescue us. And God did, quite dramatically.

After five long years of paperwork and payments, I arrived at the office to find a thick manila envelope on my desk from an attorney in Maryland. I read, page by page, my eyes widening. She was an estate attorney who was notifying us that her client had died and left all his assets to us—some cash and some property, all to be liquidated. After a few phone calls, we determined the estimated total value to be three million dollars! Who was this benefactor? We combed through decades of giving records. His name never appeared on any of them, not once. He had never attended an event, never written us a note. But he had attended our university for one year, fifty years ago, during which time—a relative informed us—he had a significant spiritual awakening. Once our jubilation stilled, I got curious. When did he sign this intent with his attorney? Thumbing through papers, I found the answer: two months after we committed ourselves to righting a wrong that no auditor had discovered or demanded we correct. Our debt was paid in full—case closed.

Here is a mystery that matters: God rewards financial integrity during the risks of leadership.

Paul Stewarded the Money Mystery

Money is a potent topic, both emotionally and theologically. Terry Munday reports that in the Bible there are 100 verses on prayer and 500 on faith—but 2,300 on money. For example, Jesus said, "Do not store up for yourselves treasures on earth, where moths and vermin destroy, and where thieves break in and steal. But store up for yourselves treasures in heaven, where moths and vermin do not destroy, and where thieves do not break in and steal. For where your treasure is, there your heart will be also" (Matt. 6:19–21). But here's the rub: only 27 percent of Christians tithe. Munday's point is, "We don't trust God with our money."[1] If we did all tithe, there would be eighty-five billion dollars available for kingdom work, annually.

Dutch Catholic priest, psychologist, and Harvard professor Henri Nouwen writes, "The reason for the taboo about money is it has to do with that intimate place in our heart where we need security and we do not want to give it away to someone who might betray us."[2]

In fact, greater wealth does not necessarily correlate to emotional security about the future. Andy Stanley writes, "Hope often accompanies riches. That's just a fact. But placing your hope *in* riches is something different. And that's where Paul draws an important line. It's one thing to have hope *and* riches, but it's another thing to have hope *in* riches. When riches become the basis for your hope—the source of it—you're headed down a slippery slope."[3] Ultimately, putting our hope in our riches constrains generosity, even among the wealthy. Having lots of money doesn't make one good at being rich any more than having lots of children makes one good at parenting. Stanley says rich people are bad at being rich because they don't practice generosity. "Isn't it strange?" he asks. "You miss money you waste or poorly invest, but you never miss money given to meet a need in someone's life. As Paul says, it is a contentment that brings great gain."[4]

The apostle Paul teaches a lot about money, and indicates a mystery that matters about generosity in particular. But let's first look at foundational money principles. First, though he is a missionary, incurring costs of travel while waiving security from a steady job, he teaches that we should live self-sufficiently. "Make it your ambition to lead a quiet life: You should mind your own business and work with your hands, just as we told you, so that your daily life may win the respect of outsiders and so that you will not be dependent on anybody" (1 Thess. 4:11–12). Further, Paul says, "We were not idle when we were with you, nor did we eat anyone's food without paying for it. On the contrary, we worked night and day, laboring and toiling so that we would not be a burden to any of you. We did this, not because we do not have the right to such help, but in order to offer ourselves as a model for you to imitate" (2 Thess. 3:7b–9).

Second, Paul teaches us to live contentedly, even with modest means. "I know what it is to be in need, and I know what it is to have plenty. I have learned the secret of being content in any and every situation, whether well fed or hungry, whether living in plenty or in want. I can do all this through him who gives me strength" (Phil. 4:12–13).

Third, Paul preaches discipline. Financial decisions would be just one application for that principle. "I strike a blow to my body and make it my slave so that after I have preached to others, I myself will not be disqualified for the prize" (1 Cor. 9:27). His word for "strike a blow" in the Greek, *hypopiazo,* means "to wear down, beat, discipline." Imagine a person who catches himself daydreaming too often while studying, and when he becomes alert gently smacks himself in the face out of frustration with his laxity, saying to himself, "C'mon, Gregg! Stick with this!" When Paul says, "I strike a blow to my body and make it my slave," he is saying that, just as a person who is tempted by lust might put a porn-blocking app on his smartphone, so will a person who lacks a financial margin do whatever it takes to live within their means, like cutting up credit cards and using cash-only envelopes for budgeting weekly purchases. Maintaining discipline assures Paul he will not "disqualify"—*adokimos*, meaning to lose authenticity by acting in ways counterfeit of the gospel. In short, Paul is saying a disciplined life is prize-worthy, rewardable, and therefore highly motivating. No doubt, this kind of financial discipline is why deacons could be entrusted to properly allocate funds to widows (Acts 6:1–6). They already qualified for this trust by managing their own households well (1 Tim. 3:8–13).

Fourth, and finally, with the financial foundations laid for self-sufficiency, contentment, and discipline of body and mind, let's now encounter a mystery that matters: God rewards financial integrity, including generosity to others, and often returns it to us in material and immaterial blessings.

There is in Scripture a prevailing assumption toward regular financial generosity, not sporadic giving. Though Paul calls for sporadic, special-use gifts for projects like a mission to Jerusalem (1 Cor. 16:2–3), he also reminds the church that those who serve the gospel full-time should find their livelihood from regular giving (1 Cor. 9:11–14). When that regular giving is 10 percent of our income, we call that "tithe." Paul further commends the Macedonian churches for the spirit in which they give. These people demonstrate "overflowing joy" despite "extreme poverty," giving financially "beyond their ability" to the needs of others (2 Cor. 8:1–3)! He sets them up as a model, explaining how "they urgently pleaded with us for the privilege of sharing in this service to the Lord's people" (v. 4). What is the lesson? We should excel not only in faith, speech, knowledge, and earnestness, but "see that you also excel in this grace of giving" (v. 7)—what modern church calls tithes and offerings.

The amount of an offering is less important than its proportionality, "for if the willingness is there, the gift is acceptable according to what one has, not according to what one does not have" (v. 12). This is why Jesus celebrated the widow's two copper coins in comparison to larger gifts from the rich: "'Truly I tell you,' he said, 'this poor widow has put in more than all the others. All these people gave their gifts out of their wealth; but she out of her poverty put in all she had to live on'" (Luke 21:3–4). In modern nomenclature, Americans who enjoy the highest standard of living in world history—despite most never thinking of ourselves as "rich"—should not feel self-approval by putting several digits on their giving checks if that reflects only a small percentage of their income. For this reason, Paul teaches enthusiastically, "Command those who are rich in this present world not to be arrogant nor to put their hope in wealth, which is so uncertain, but to put their hope in God, who richly provides us with everything for our enjoyment. Command them to do good, to be rich in good deeds, and to be generous and willing to share" (1 Tim. 6:17–18).

The mystery to steward in this is: if we don't hoard money but share it as God directs, God's generosity returns to us! Indeed, God blesses the giver: "Give, and it will be given to you. A good measure, pressed down, shaken together and running over, will be poured into your lap. For with the measure you use, it will be measured to you" (Luke 6:38). And Paul says, "Remember this: Whoever sows sparingly will also reap sparingly, and whoever sows generously will also reap generously. Each of you should give what you have decided in your heart to give [offering, not tithe], not reluctantly or under compulsion, for God loves a cheerful giver. And God is able to bless you abundantly, so that in all things at all times, having all that you need, you will abound in every good work" (2 Cor. 9:6–8). I believe this, practice it, and experience it. Was it coincidence that, two months after my wife and I pledged a substantial sum to the building program of our church, I got a promotion and raise that equaled the value of our pledge? Nope. This is God at work. He doesn't serve me; I serve him; but he is faithful, materially and immaterially.

Stepping on the Tithing Toes

Now, a word about tithing—that is, specifically, giving 10 percent of your income to the church. Let me guess. You're feeling uncomfortable already! The truth is, the two-by-two-square-inch wallet in the pockets of Americans is the most protected real estate on earth, and among Christians, the distance between grim financial mandates and cheerful generosity is about forty miles. So I write you cautiously, reminded by Martin Luther, preaching in 1532, to differentiate salvation by works from faith: "Distinguishing between the law and the gospel is the highest art in Christendom."[5] Both are God's Word, but they are not the same doctrine. Law commands obedience while the gospel is a doctrine of grace that requires no performance, only faith. Luther said, "If at this point I fail to distinguish Moses and Christ, I cannot be free, I cannot escape, I must end in despair."[6]

The skirmish over mandatory tithing versus selective generosity is sophisticatedly debated in David Croteau's *Perspectives on Tithing*.[7] In the fourth century, Augustine did not believe the New Testament commanded Christians to tithe but to make *all* their possessions available to the poor. Believing nobody would do that, he advocated people at least imitate the Jews and give

10 percent. Tertullian, in the second century, said tithing was voluntary. In the Middle Ages, Thomas Aquinas declared tithes to be so connected to Old Testament ceremony that they were not required of New Testament believers, while Charlemagne and Bernard of Clairvaux advocated tithing. In the Reformation period, Martin Luther defended the usefulness of tithing but believed it was not binding, while Anabaptists called for the abolition of a tithing mandate yet encouraged voluntary giving. In the Post-Reformation era, Matthew Henry and Charles Finney advocated 10-percent tithing plus frequent supplemental offerings, while the Quakers so vigorously believed tithing was only for the Old Testament Levites that many went to prison for withholding. More recently, Billy Graham supported tithing while John MacArthur opposed it.

The conversation is robust and the opinions varied, but nobody defends entire withholding of financial generosity from the needs of the church and its ministries. Even those theologians who oppose the tithe only do so in its strictest sense of 10 percent. So the question for us remains, how much?! Is it more like, if an Old Testament law is not repeated in the New Testament, it is repealed? Or is it like, if an Old Testament law is not explicitly repealed, it continues?

I tithe. I always have, and so has my wife. We started as teens. I followed the example of my parents. Our adult kids tithe as well, probably because we talked about it a lot before they came into much money, establishing discipline before the stakes got high. For all our married life, my wife and I have tithed regularly with additional offerings for episodic causes, including when we were paupers—I'm talking, a family-of-five-on-$35,000-per-year kind of life. God is the source of all I have, my rescuer when I am in want, so I want my tithe to go on record with him: I owe him everything, and trust him to provide after I give.

The model of our ancestors in the faith inspires me. Abraham set the pattern, giving a tenth of his crop yield to honor God, even before the tithing system entered civil law for the Israelite people (see Gen. 14:18–20). The purpose of regular tithing is later outlined in Numbers 18, when God says to Aaron, the head of the Levitical priesthood: "I give to the Levites all the tithes in Israel as their inheritance in return for the work they do while serving at the tent of meeting" (v. 21). This system makes sense to me—that, if a pastor devotes full-time to serving the people, their sustenance is provided by the people. I've been to regions of Africa where there is no currency, but they still passed the plate, which soon filled with produce. This is why tithing could come in cash or liquidated goods (Deut. 14:22–27). We also tithe to care for the poor, through the church: "At the end of every three years, bring all the tithes of that year's produce and store it in your towns, so that the Levites (who have no allotment or inheritance of their own) and the foreigners, the fatherless and the widows who live in your towns may come and eat and be satisfied, and so that the Lord your God may bless you in all the work of your hands" (Deut. 14:28–29).

Advocates of tithing can get stern about this, saying that to withhold it is tantamount to robbing God (Mal. 3:6–12). Commandment number eight—"you shall not steal" (Exod. 20:15)—is formidable. Philip Ryken says that the Hebrew word for "steal," *ganaf*, covers all kinds of theft: breaking into a home, threatening violence and taking something directly from a person, seizing goods in transit, shoplifting, pickpocketing, embezzlement, extortion, racketeering, stealing time at work, price gouging, and usury or loan-sharking. Ryken says the eighth commandment also covers failing to tithe: "A tithe is 10 percent, and this is a useful guideline for Christian giving," Ryken says, because, while "God does not operate on a percentage basis . . . to give less than we can is spiritual theft"[8] against God and others. Every theft is a failure to trust in God's provision and is an assault on God's providence for others, robbing what God has provided for them through us.

Notably, Jesus does not repeal the tithe in his instruction to the religious elite: "Woe to you, teachers of the law and Pharisees, you hypocrites! You give a tenth of your spices—mint, dill and cumin. But you have neglected the more important matters of the law—justice, mercy and faithfulness. You should have practiced the latter, without neglecting the former" (Matt. 23:23). In other words, kindness is not a substitute for tithing. Your large tip to a waitress, or buying out the full stock of Girl Scout cookies, or paying for your neighbor child's private school is very generous. Terrific! But that is not a tithe—if it were, no congregations or ministerial staff could exist, and the needs of the poor would be even less met.

However, there are smart and sincere people who challenge a strict observance of tithing: to give anywhere from 1 percent to 9.5 percent may not be sin, and can miss the point of financial stewardship. Let's hear them out too. These advocates say that codifying Old Testament practices into modern life can mistreat Scripture. Many sections of the Bible were not written *to us* specifically but are still *for us* generally. For example, if we insist on a 10-percent tithe from Old Testament principles, why do we not also insist on the supplemental festival and charity tithes, combining to 23 percent annually? And, though Jacob promises God 10 percent in Genesis 28, it is conditional upon God's blessing him in the future—and there is no commentary on whether that is a singular episode for Jacob or a new and regular giving discipline. Meanwhile, Jews outside of Palestine did not tithe—only those in God's nation of Israel.

When Paul says, "For sin shall no longer be your master, because you are not under the law, but under grace" (Rom. 6:14), he reminds us that the civil laws governed the nation of Israel specifically and provided ceremonial laws for religious festivals generally (Exod. 23:14–19) and that neither is in effect anymore because all those regulations aimed to satisfy God in the way now accomplished on the cross by Jesus. God's people once did atonement sacrifices of animals for their sin, but we no longer need to because Jesus was the supreme sacrifice for sin, and our faith in him and in his act is what constitutes righteousness, not our efforts (Rom. 3:28).

So this perspective says, look for the moral content of an Old Testament tithing practice rather than transactional, performative obedience and, in so doing, more fully embody its purpose, altering your motivations. The purpose of the law was to make us aware of sin (Rom. 3:20), but our righteousness can never be proved in surrendering 10 percent; God cannot be bought. Instead, the moral content of the law puts us in a kind of social contract with God through our conscience. This is why Jesus does not cancel the law but interiorizes it in the Sermon on the Mount. He encourages us to examine the outward focus of the law and turn it inward, transforming the state of our hearts (Matt. 5–7).

So, now we change the question from, "Must I give 10 percent to appease God?" to "What can I give?"—which could exceed 10 percent. We must be emotionally prepared to follow through when we receive an uncomfortable answer from God. This is why the rich young ruler sulked away after being told to diminish the self-righteousness of keeping rules and sell all his possessions to follow God (Mark 10:17–27).

As we give, Paul reminds us of a mystery that matters: God blesses us, sometimes in material ways and other times in immaterial ways (2 Cor. 9:6–15). We realign our motivations from giving because we *must* or giving toward a mathematical formula, to giving because we *can*, and are on mission with Jesus to meet the needs of the church. The idea that God rewards financial integrity is not a health-and-wealth gospel. It's not "give so you get back." Instead, it is what Ryken calls an inside-out rule: What is demanded externally implies the need for inward change.[9] The most basic notion of financial generosity to others is that we trust a promise on the credibility of the Promiser. To give cheerfully, not transactionally, keeps the moral content of money central. What a joy to give in proportion to what you have, and be "pleased to do it" (Rom. 15:27).

Money in a Leader's Hands: Corporate Generosity

Not all projects are monetized. If yours is, start considering how corporate generosity differs from personal generosity. Have you noticed that people demand far greater rationality from organizations than personal relationships? Corporate actions have corporate effects. Virtually every decision is subject to critique. This makes a leader—despite title, stature, or authority—more prime minister than queen. We who lead still must cultivate a constituency around what our team or organization is doing, motivating with *why*.

As one guy told me, "The higher you climb the ladder of success, the more your fanny is exposed to everyone!" This is especially true about money in the hands of leaders—not just operational budgets but also patterns of corporate generosity. As A. W. Tozer writes, "Somebody observed about Christopher Columbus, 'Columbus went out not knowing where he was going; and when he got there he did not know where he was; and when he got back he did not know where he had been, and he did it all on other people's money.'"[10] It's one thing to add several zeros to your own personal check, but should you tip 40 percent on a corporate card? No—because the morality of generosity requires personal sacrifice. Tossing out shillings from your expense account might bless the waiter, but it is no substitute for personal giving. Also, corporate generosity in a private, for-profit company or a nonprofit organization can look to a financially strapped employee like you are squandering their raise. And if you're a publicly traded company, those expenses diminish profitability and return on investment (ROI), making any form of corporate generosity more accountable. Corporate giving, therefore, requires more systematic thinking than personal philanthropy, funneling funds into predetermined causes, more explicitly expressed from mission and values, taking into account timing and scale. Effectively, this becomes budgeted generosity.

Nassim Taleb helps us understand how companies can be most honorable in giving. His book is titled *Skin in the Game*, a reference to the colloquialism that means sharing risk in a transaction. If you don't pay a penalty when something goes wrong, you have no skin in the game; if you don't risk, you shouldn't see reward. But when deals are structured with high stakes for both parties, it lights a fire under everyone's feet, making all parties run faster. Focus, intensity, and outcomes change. There is, of course, a sliding scale here. It is honorable to refrain from doing some things regardless of material rewards, such as prostitution, or to do some things unconditionally, like sacrificing one's life to preserve a child's.

The most honorable thing is putting your own skin in the game for the benefit of others. Taleb illustrates: (1) The structure of some professions leaves no skin in the game, like financial advisors who get paid regardless of market performance, business consultants getting paid regardless of whether their advice works, or lawmakers retaining office even if they accomplish nothing. (2) Other professions have skin in the game for their own benefit, such as investors or private merchants. (3) The most honorable are those with skin in the game for others—philanthropists, prophets, soldiers.[11]

A person stewarding the mystery can convert any domain, expanding honor by adding skin in the game for others. For example, a financial advisor can help a client grow wealth for the expressed purpose of increased philanthropy. A business consultant could actually invest his own funds in the initiative for which he consults. A merchant can budget corporate giving as a percentage of profits: TOMS Shoes, for example, does this by donating a new pair of shoes for each pair sold.

So it comes to this: somebody has to decide if generosity is a purpose of your project. "The secret of leadership is simple," say Henry and Richard Blackaby. "Do what you believe in. Paint a picture of the future. Go there. People will follow. . . . It is one part hindsight, one part insight, one part foresight, and a healthy dose of chutzpah!"[12] So decide! Is generosity in your vision for your project?

Giving and Getting—to Give

Despite the fourfold financial trauma I described in the beginning of this chapter, we decided to maintain corporate generosity where possible. Such a joy it was to bring Irene before a large group, publicly congratulating her as a forty-five-year custodian. Her hands had touched every room in every building, supporting thousands of people over the course of her career. Despite our financial pain, we scraped through our budgets to present her with patio furniture at her retirement party.

Then imagine it: a student's car caught on fire in the parking lot, and that was a replacement for her prior one, which had died just two months earlier! So we cooked up a fun idea. One of my colleagues managed a small donation fund for urgent student needs. We had not used it in a while, so the account had grown to $4,000. One of our trustees owned a car dealership. He graciously sold us a quality, used car at wholesale cost. We called the student up front during chapel and had her face the congregation while we told her story. Meanwhile a few bulky staff men rolled the car from the stage wings to a halt a few feet behind where she stood. It felt like *The Price Is Right*!

In another setting, we caught a student being honest in the bookstore. She had four siblings in a household held together by a modest family business, so pocket money didn't come easily. One day she shopped our apparel section, spotted a sweatshirt, and took it off the rack with excitement. But as she pivoted toward the cash register, she noticed that all the same items on the rack were priced much higher than the one in her hands. With integrity, she surrendered the item to the clerk, saying, "I could afford it at the price marked, but it must be an error because all the other ones are marked higher. You should probably fix that." Then she left the store. Later on we brought her up in front of a group, gave her the item in question, and then a donor who loves to reward integrity provided ten hundred-dollar bills. We called out each bill one by one and watched her eyes bulge.

What do these acts of corporate generosity accomplish during financial duress? They demonstrate to God that we trust him, not our bank account. Not only did we see that $3M estate fund cover our debt, but another $15M came to us in a subsequent fundraising campaign. But that is just cash. Many non-monetary blessings came too, like a good name, high-quality employees, affirmation from accreditors, and students packed around the altar from the gift of the Holy Spirit. What would you pay for that? Yes, in this is a mystery that matters.

Your Turn

Jonathan Haidt, an atheist moral philosopher, says that communities with religious purpose survive longer than communities with secular purpose and that religious Americans are more generous to the needy with their time and money.[13] If your project holds a Godward purpose, and you put financial skin in the game for others, your cause may endure longer than others, even against forces to undermine it.

It's your turn to steward the mystery that God rewards financial integrity. If your project is monetized, take these steps with your team to determine a corporate giving plan, or if the project doesn't involve money, you can still make a personal giving plan from these prompts.

Identifying a Philanthropic Cause

R. Mark Dillon says that "philanthropy" in Greek literally means to love humankind.[14] So when we try to decide where to give, we are deciding whom to love. Reader, whom do you want to love with philanthropy from your project? In *The Art of Being Unreasonable*, Eli Broad developed criteria to help him answer that question. As the only American in history to launch companies in different industries and grow them to Fortune 500s

(KB Homes and Sun America), this billionaire now transfers his competition for stock price, market share, and profitability to compete against himself each year in growing his philanthropic impact. By these three questions he assesses whether he should provide funding: (1) Will it matter in twenty years? (2) Would it happen even if I weren't involved? and (3) Do we have the right people in place to make this happen?[15]

So here's your question: What do you absolutely love to see happen for other people? Using Broad's criteria, which cause gets on your radar? Talk about it with your project team. You might find calibration between this domain of thinking and the calling or spiritual gifts identified in your team from chapter 4.

Dreaming about Scale

We never change until God penetrates the structure of our imagination. Let's start dreaming about how to love humankind at a large scale, through the proceeds of your project. Name an aspirational annual goal (in dollars) for corporate philanthropy. Your team might toss out wildly different numbers, from hundreds to hundreds of thousands of dollars. That's okay at this step. The most important thing is to get dreaming!

Budgeting Philanthropy

One way to reduce conflict over how much to give is to plan for philanthropy in your budget. Scan your project budget to see where you could operate more frugally to create the financial capacity for corporate philanthropy. Then make a donation budget!

Giving Intervals or Spontaneous Work?

Talk with your team about how to structure your giving. A high-structure plan would be budgeting specific philanthropic amounts as a percentage of quarterly profits, with the dollar figure determined the first day of each quarter. A more flexible approach is to let the philanthropic budget line grow until someone on the project team finds a compelling need and pitches the idea with varying frequency.

To Board or Not to Board?

If the scale of your philanthropic plans is big and the range of causes broad, you can focus impact by structuring a foundation board that accumulates funds over longer periods of time and never spends the corpus but invests it in the markets so that your philanthropic spend is on the annual investment return. That board can also be vested with authority to receive all giving proposals and vet them against expressed criteria to determine the highest impact associated with your philanthropic mission.

Tax Considerations

Your mechanism of giving could save you massive funds by IRS rules, such as: (a) donating an asset before it is liquidated (no capital gains tax), and (b) claiming the donation on your annual taxes. Capital gains are the profits from the sale of an asset—shares of stock, a piece of land, a business—and generally are considered taxable income. A lot depends on how long you held the asset before selling. For example, if you sold a stock for a $10,000 profit this year and sold another at a $4,000 loss, you'll be taxed on capital gains of $6,000. The difference between your capital gains and your capital losses is called your "net capital gain." In recent years, capital gains tax rates have been 0%, 15%, or 20% for most assets held for more than a year, but if held for less than a year, taxes will correspond to ordinary income tax brackets. But if you donate the asset, there are no capital gains taxes.

Perhaps by now, you are ready to steward this financial mystery that matters. But one thing more certain than death and taxes is this: a team of people surrounding money and mission decisions will produce conflict. Paul stewarded a mystery for that too. Chapter 6 might help.

SIX
CONFRONTATION, NOT AVOIDANCE, BRINGS PEACE

Everyone experiences relational conflict. It is our part of the human condition. But how many face it well? As I was typing this—no kidding!—a colleague informed me that a member of his team had stormed out of a session, leaving everyone confused.

This chapter does not tinker with low-scale conflict over whether to eat chicken or fish, or if the carpet should be blue or green. Rather, it focuses on high-stakes issues that are marked by strong emotion and clashing opinions—the kinds of issues that caused Paul to traverse some of the hottest conflict domains: nonprofits and religion. The authors of the bestselling book *Crucial Conversations* learned from studying 2,200 projects involving 100,000 people which conflict-management behaviors are necessary to keep the peace under strain.

You know the moment it happens. "In a matter of minutes," they say, "an innocent discussion had transformed into a failed conversation, and you can't recall why. You remember a tense moment when you started pushing your point of view a bit too hard, and eight people stared at you as if you just bit off the head of a chicken. Then the meeting ended. What you don't realize is two of your friends walk down the hallway in the opposite direction, conducting a play-by-play of the meeting, and they do know what took place."[1]

But companies whose people engage conflict skillfully experience five-times-faster financial recovery during a downturn, are two-thirds more likely to avoid injury during unsafe conditions, and avoid up to thirteen different forms of drag on a project's momentum from gossip, backstabbing, undermining, and passive aggression. Stephen M. R. Covey provides a detailed typology of conflict scenarios in *The Speed of Trust*, where the lowest-trust relationships produce the highest tax on an organization, and high-trust groups enjoy great "dividends."[2]

Notably, the worst condition with the highest dysfunction is quiet, not loud. A nonexistent trust environment could be marked by loud and angry confrontations but more often is cold and bitter, marked by quiet withdrawal. In my experience, many Christians use silence as violence. People confuse attitudinal injunctions in the Bible to turn the other cheek (Matt. 5:38–40) or to forgive seventy times seven (Matt. 18:21–22) as directives to evade confrontation. As my wife says, "Ignoring conflict is false peace-making." Drop the mic. Tweet that. Or, to put it another way, if you won't come to the table of remedy, you'll be on the menu!

Even when the practice isn't complete silence, trouble brews. A wounded person finds an ally to seek confirmation of their perspective, rather than confronting the offender. This behavior can compound the issue by embittering the third party toward the offender. There is no courage, skill, or integrity in this action. As the writer of Proverbs says, "Enemies disguise themselves with their lips, but in their hearts they harbor deceit" (26:24). To avoid or ignore does not erase reality but drives it underground. As my farmer and pastor grandfather understood from working agriculture and shepherding people, whatever you press down into dark soil will grow! This circumvention tactic worsens conflict, ironically in the name of turn-the-other-cheek Christianity.

Then, of course, this friction in a dyad metastasizes across the entire department or organization. Covey says that where trust is low and conflict high, expect redundant work, cumbersome and slow bureaucracy, power-seeking politics, disengagement where people effectively resign on the inside while keeping their jobs, turnover spikes in employees *and* customers, and the worst settings even experience sabotage, obstruction, and disruption. This is not an exaggeration. My neighbor, several years ago, explained how union-management conflicts at his General Motors plant inspired workers to break the equipment, slowing production as a negotiation tactic.

So c'mon, people: confront! Let's not get it twisted. The same Jesus who stares meekly from your framed painting in the living room also challenged folks! In Matthew 5:23–24, he says if your conscience stirs about a conflict while you are at the altar, you should leave the offering and get reconciled. Note this command has nothing to do with who is right. More strongly, when Jesus sees corruption, he takes the time to make his own whip in preparation to flip over tables and drive people out of the temple (see John 2:13–17). In viewing hypocrisy, he calls the Pharisees hypocrites, children of hell, blind guides, fools, whitewashed tombs that look good on the outside but are dead inside, and snakes (see Matt. 23:15, 16, 17, 27, 33).

Christian psychologist Rick Sorensen reminds us of this paradox. The same merciful, forgiving, peace-loving Jesus remained, during these out-bursts, God-in-the-flesh (Col. 2:9), a righteous judge (2 Tim. 4:8), not vola-tile but in fact one who always does what the Father directs (John 8:29). Jesus is expressing out of the same godhead who killed three thousand Israelites for worshiping a golden calf while the law was being given to Moses (Exod. 32); who sent a plague to kill twenty-four thousand Israelites for sexual im-morality and worshiping a false god of the Moabites (Num. 25); and who destroyed the entire population of earth in the great flood due to rampant sin (Gen. 7).[3] Yet Jesus is, of course, also the Messiah, self-sacrificial Lamb of God (John 1:29), who forgives all our sin (Matt. 9:4–8) and restores us to righteousness (1 John 1:9).

Hmm. How can we navigate this quandary? Blameless wrath with righ-teous mercy? Clearing the temple without sinning in our anger? The apostle Paul discerned this. Despite his intense anguish in conflict, even to the point of tears, he learned a procedure we need. In this he stewarded the mystery that confrontation of a certain sort—not avoidance—brings peace.

Conflict Hard on You? Paul Too!

A theme in this book is that Paul is a more relatable figure than we think. Not only can we cultivate competence for the Spirit-led life, just like Paul, without ever encountering the material Jesus, but we can also do it in human weakness, as he did. In fact, conflict is hard on Paul, just as it is hard on us. It gives him "great sorrow and unceasing anguish" (Rom. 9:2) and causes him to write "out of great distress and anguish of heart and with many tears" (2 Cor. 2:4). Yet he feels responsible to intervene, making sure to "warn those who are idle and disruptive, encourage the disheartened, help the weak, be patient with everyone" and to "make sure that nobody pays back wrong for wrong" (1 Thess. 5:14b, 15a). For example, he begs the followers Euodia and Syntyche to agree with each other, "to be of the same mind in the Lord" (Phil. 4:2). Addressing the quarrels in the Corinthian church, reported to him by "some from Chloe's household" (1 Cor. 1:11), he urges "that all of you agree with one another in what you say and that there be no divisions among you, but that you be perfectly united" (1 Cor. 1:10).

Of course, Paul isn't mediating low-scale conflict over what to eat for dinner. He is operating in the toughest domain. Maybe your project fits that category too. Religion and politics tend to be the highest-stakes conflicts of our culture because they are moral domains, and to question a person's opinion is tantamount to questioning their identity or character.

Jonathan Haidt explains that religious conflict is not ultimately a cerebral affair but is governed by snap moral judgments based on intuition. This process is not "rational thought in search of truth, but a reasoning process to support one's emotional reaction." Think of it, he says, like your mind is the rider atop your emotional animal, struggling to guide it. No matter how much the rider protests, emotion rules like an elephant, dominating the rider by its power, very slow to move or change, and with a long memory. However, this rider-elephant dynamic, in practice during conflict, is dignified—more like lawyer-client than servant-master. But, "if you want to change a person's mind, you've got to talk to their elephant," not primarily to the rider.[4]

Yes, Paul's fights certainly qualify as crucial conversations (high stakes, diverse opinions, strong emotions). It is doctrinal stuff. One is over whether a gentile who comes to faith should be circumcised like the Jews (see Acts 15). Hey, fellas, we definitely don't want a conflict avoider on that one! Paul also mediates fights over holy days (Rom. 14), which foods to eat (1 Cor. 8), and how to operate Communion (1 Cor. 11).

Okay, so maybe your project team isn't faced with religious or political strife, but yours might be nestled in another landscape with peculiar challenges: operating a nonprofit organization. My dissertation research examined the differences between how workers in nonprofit and for-profit contexts experience anxiety-producing change. I compared middle management for General Motors to private-school teachers because both groups cope with onerous quality standards imposed by external forces. The result was that nonprofit employees produce more communication "noise" while coping with pressure and change than the for-profit folks, for three reasons.

First, employees use their nonprofit as a way to express their identity, so any change that threatens its mission or values cuts deeper and may be resisted harder. Second, nonprofits have fewer objective standards for success than for-profit organizations, so changes in nonprofits produce more squabbling in review of the threat potential for change, while for-profit employees reach satisfaction with change earlier because the impact—the bottom line—can more immediately be known. Third, many—though not all—nonprofits depend heavily on volunteers to deliver goods and services. Tolerance of change by the unpaid shortens the lifespan of patience, leading to a higher volunteer or employee turnover.[5]

Another dimension of Paul's context compounds his difficulty with conflict, and might fit your project scale in some way. His leadership spans a large, multisite effort. This itinerant evangelist recruits and manages leaders across different cities, countries, and cultures. That level of leadership magnifies conflict. D. Michael Lindsay reports as much in *View From The Top*—the largest U.S. study of high-profile leaders. Senior leaders spend a majority of time in two categories often blind to the workforce or general public: working extra hours to keep bad news from becoming public scandals, and working on big, bold things that never materialize. Inside those scandals is relational conflict. When asked about the hardest decisions they make, 41 percent—the highest ranking in a plurality of topics, in fact ranking double in scale as the next most common item—America's most senior leaders say the hardest issues are personnel conflicts![6]

Yes, Paul lived it, just like we do. But how grateful we are that he stewarded the mystery, modeling for us that to confront conflict in a particular way, not avoid it, brings peace.

Attitude before Confrontation

Before we prescribe how to do conflict confrontation, let's set an attitude that pleases God and follows Paul's model. First, Paul teaches a principle that is either unpopular or misunderstood in modern time, and we must get it straight: in order to maintain the purity of the church, believers are to *judge* other believers. "But now I am writing to you that you must not associate with anyone who claims to be a brother or sister but is sexually immoral or greedy, an idolater or slanderer, a drunkard or swindler. Do not even eat with such people. What business is it of mine to judge those outside the church? Are you not to judge those inside? God will judge those outside. 'Expel the wicked person from among you'" (1 Cor. 5:11–13). So, if you have believers on your project team, they are fair game, and so are you!

Paul goes further by clarifying the almost thoughtless default mantra of our time: "judge not." We must not distort the words of Jesus in Matthew 7. We are not to operate in universal acceptance of any opinion or lifestyle but should acknowledge the obvious fact that every life is known by its fruit. Some people relate in ways that yield bad fruit, and must be confronted about it! However, while addressing another's attitudes or actions, maintain a motive and tone that are not superior. We can show unconditional love, remaining in the constant-ready state to receive another who seeks peace, but offer conditional approval. That is why Paul teaches the Corinthians to disassociate from believers whose hypocrisy endures after confrontation. The caution is to be fair in defining the standards, such that you also meet them.

With this encouragement to confrontation, Paul also teaches an attitude by which we do it that is marked by self-examination. During conflict, most of us persuade ourselves of our own innocence, convinced of our virtue. But it is possible we trick ourselves! For even if I satisfy my own conscience, that does not necessarily mean I am innocent (see 1 Cor. 4:4). The psalmist helps us understand that God's concern is not only with outward and obvious sin but also with our hidden faults (Ps. 19:12). I think this is why Paul also teaches us to not think too highly of ourselves (Rom. 12:3) and to consider others ahead of ourselves (Phil. 2:3).

Archie Brown underscores the importance of this leadership posture in *The Myth of the Strong Leader*, calling us away from our assessment of leaders within the weak-strong dichotomy, as if we are weightlifters or marathon runners, and toward strengths as relaters. Though leadership strength must be advertised to rise to any office of significance, that is not what keeps a person there. Their skills and character traits do: skills like intelligence, shrewdness, comprehension, and energy; character traits like integrity, curiosity, seeking disparate views, courage, and empathy. Some leaders get preoccupied with power, believing themselves to hold special insight and viewing the organization as an arena in which to exercise their forcefulness. Lasting leaders, however, embrace problems pragmatically in a non-self-referential manner. Brown quotes Max Weber's words about politicians, but they could apply to any leader: "Daily and hourly, a [leader] has to overcome a quite vulgar vanity . . . constantly in danger of becoming an actor, concerned, above all, with the impression that he is making."[7] So just do good work—without peacocking.

We could adopt the approach Paul demonstrates by mentoring his protégé, Timothy. On low-level conflict, "Don't have anything to do with foolish and stupid arguments, because you know they produce quarrels" (2 Tim. 2:23). But on crucial conversations (the ones with high stakes, varying opinions, and strong emotions), what did Paul say in the very next verses? "Gently instruct" the other. That is *paideuonta* in Greek, "to raise up, educate with discipline." In this context, we help another become mature and responsible about their toxic impact. And the purpose of that confrontation, according to Paul, is so "that they will come to their senses," *ananepsosin*, get sober-minded about what is really going on.

Here is a mystery that matters in conflict: once our attitude for confrontation holds a high view of the other, is reflective about our hidden faults, and strives for gentleness, it is more likely—though not certain—to produce lasting peace from godly sorrow, in contrast to fleeting, worldly sorrow (2 Cor.

7:8–13). Paul is saying that, although the act of confrontation is painful, ultimately it makes him "happy, not because you were made sorry, but because your sorrow led you to repentance" (v. 9). The markers of godly sorrow are alarm at the awareness of the damage you've done, eagerness to patch things up, and readiness to act in justice. But worldly sorrow is this simple: phoning in an apology to pacify the confronter so you can get on with your life.

On our university campus, we see this dichotomy so often that it factors into our redemptive discipline plan. In many circumstances, a sincere and repentant response justifies softer punishment. Recently, we had a very sensitive one. Despite our multi-pronged agenda to remedy racial strife and promote racial equity, it pained us to learn that a white student had written the N-word on the dry-erase message board that hung on the hallway door of a black resident assistant. The RA wanted to deescalate, requesting that if the offender confessed and apologized, no university discipline be enacted. We were thrilled to see that very thing occur the next day. We chose to honor the RA's gracious leadership and not punish. Unfortunately, the offender betrayed himself by using the same word, in a different setting and in a joking manner, only two weeks later. Now, we realized, his sorrow had been worldly and not godly. We suspended him for three days and put him on social probation to inspire godly sorrow. That woke him up for more permanent change.

A Confrontation Methodology

Now that we have set up the proper attitude toward confrontation, we need a process. Like Paul said, "Anyone who competes as an athlete does not receive the victor's crown except by competing according to the rules. Reflect on what I am saying, for the Lord will give you insight into all this" (2 Tim. 2:5, 7). So what are the rules for confrontation? Jesus instructs a four-step sequence, later echoed and elaborated by Paul, with such escalating accountability that most conflicts can be settled by the second step. All of this is applicable to your project team. Use it! Unfortunately, I've faced issues that required all four steps. In Matthew 18:15–20 the Messiah lays this out for us, with nearly identical language from Paul in 1 Cor. 5:9–13; 2 Cor. 13:1; 2 Thess. 3:14; and Titus 3:10.

First, "go and point out their fault, just between the two of you. If they listen to you, you have won them over" (Matt. 18:15). This basic step is often forgotten! Many times I have people lobby me to intervene for the offenses of another, but when I ask if they explained to the offender the effect of their actions, I get a lot of blank stares. It's not that this idea never occurred to them. But they skip it because it's hard, and people too often lack the courage, skill, or integrity to actually do it!

Second, "But if they will not listen, take one or two others along, so that 'every matter may be established by the testimony of two or three witnesses'" (v. 16). This helps you skip your impulse toward strangulation and instead use triangulation! You know how it works: when you are one on one, the perception or interpretation of an ignorant or toxic person can run askew. A third party can provide the credibility and force of shared judgment, grounding the issue in reality. Note that this arrangement is an entirely different category than what we already condemned—seeking support from a third party without ever confronting the offender.

I'll never forget the day our three elementary-through-junior-high kids huddled in the corner of the kitchen, whispering while I cooked dinner. It had been about two years since my wife, Tammy, had gone back into full-time teaching, so I picked up the Monday–Friday grocery and dinner prep. Apparently two years was enough. Yes, I heard my kids complain about some of my dishes, but I never changed the recipe until that fateful day when all three marched toward me with purpose and confidence on their faces.

"Dad," said our eldest, Abbey, speaking for the group, "you're fired." Indeed, a testimony of witnesses brought change that isolated complaints never could!

But I've been on the other side of the equation in more serious work situations, and the method is just as reliable. It sounds like this: "Jim, I invited the Human Resources director with me today because it seems multiple approaches by your team haven't found traction, and my sense is that the director and I share the concern. How can we work with you to resolve this situation with your team?"

The third step is this: "If they still refuse to listen, tell it to the church" (v. 17a). Some of you may be cocking your head right now, either because your project team doesn't function in the context of Christian membership and purpose—or, if it does, you just bugged your eyes out like a cartoon. Does this sound bizarre? Yes, only because it is so rarely needed or practiced. If your team isn't composed of believers, think of this stage as taking it to the full work team, or if that team is large, to a panel of high-integrity intercessors.

The Greek word Jesus uses for "refuse to listen" is *parakouo* (Matt. 18:17), which means to reject counsel or even blatantly disobey. So we're not talking about going public on someone who accepts your invitation to talk and still does not agree with you but remains open for continued dialogue. We're talking about a person who basically gives you the finger, or short of that, effectively refuses to meet for reconciliation. Where does the accountability go? The Greek word for "church" is *ekklesia*, meaning the "company of Christians" or "congregation." Some commentators interpret this to mean that we should go to church authorities like pastors, bishops, deacons, elders, or church boards because, the larger the congregation, the more chaotic, variant, or perhaps disunified will be the counsel. The reasoning goes that if deacons, for example, already meet the biblical criteria as outlined by Paul (1 Tim. 3:8–13), they should be entrusted with representing the whole body. Or, in the case of a project team without believers, you need a panel of representatives who are of the highest integrity and credibility. So you can see if, after even this more public accountability in stage three, the person still defies an admonition, he effectively excommunicates himself.

I saw the fruit of this procedure. Our small group leader at church was a paid staff member and was found to have breached sexual ethics with a woman who was not his spouse. Although the relationship did not grow fully into a consummated affair, the behavior was immoral. This man confessed once he was approached one on one by an overseer, then confessed to his wife, then to the senior pastor, who terminated his employment. This language may sound odd, but it was almost beautiful to witness two more steps—for the purity of transparency, accountability, and courage. I was in the room when this man stood before our group with his wife, described in strategically vague yet not evasive language what had transpired, and apologized. An hour later, the senior pastor addressed our Sunday morning congregation to convey the delicate news. Ironically, the man exited our fellowship with honor. How many do you know who would do this? Normally, the offender entrenches further because they remain unchastened through the botched management of steps 1–3. Or, as is more often the case, the callousness of their guilt proves impenetrable.

The fourth step is, "And if they refuse to listen even to the church, treat them as you would a pagan or a tax collector" (Matt. 18:17b). Paul echoes, "Take special note of anyone who does not obey our instruction in this letter. Do not associate with them, in order that they may feel ashamed" (2 Thess. 3:14). Now, if your project team has no Christian membership or purpose, then the fourth step is clearly employment-termination time. But what about a volunteer? Ostracize them. Shun them. Don't meet with them. Don't invite them to your gatherings. Stop reaching out entirely. This doesn't sound like the meek-faced Messiah staring down from the framed painting on your wall, does it?

Why culminate conflict with this extraordinary maneuver? Paul plainly provides the motive—"in order that they may feel ashamed." Paul's Greek word for "ashamed" is *entrepo*, "to confound and turn them around." This approach is meant to produce a potent emotional response in the category of, "What?! Are you kidding me?!" Answer: yes, the conflict is that serious. The same word is used in Titus 2:7–8: "In everything set them an example by doing what is good. In your teaching show integrity, seriousness and soundness of speech that cannot be condemned, so that those who oppose you may be ashamed because they have nothing bad to say about us." Indeed, to confound someone speechless is a powerful motivator. But God's conditional blessing is never detached from unconditional love. The offender and victim remain in a constant-ready state to welcome and forgive those who seek it, which is why Paul finishes the teaching this way: "Yet do not regard them as an enemy, but warn them as you would a fellow believer" (2 Thes. 3:15). If you win them over, be quick to forgive the grievance (Col. 3:13).

Yes, I've witnessed this very rare procedure too. Frankly, it was the painful culmination of four long years of stages one, two, and three. I couldn't believe we had to resort to it, but the offender simply would not moderate themselves, no matter how we tried. We provided analogies, articles, set up teleconferences with experts, brought into the living room credible accomplices. Indeed, the only strategy that finally inspired change was social estrangement. But praise the Lord! The pain of shunning motivated an otherwise evasive reconciliation.

Confrontation Content

With a foundation now set for a biblical attitude and process, let's make a content plan for confrontation. Best practices come from the *Crucial Conversations* authors and their research. I used this format several times. These tips decrease ambiguity over what to say, increase confidence from planning, and show a high success rate in generating conflict resolution.[8] I add one precursor that is not explicated by the authors: show courtesy by setting a meeting a few days in advance, and name the purpose so the other is emotionally prepared and does not feel attacked. It is important for high-stakes issues to be given adequate time. My sense is that, three times out of four, a confrontation yields only partial value simply for lack of establishing the time and topic in advance of the encounter. For example: "Sarah, I have been disappointed with [name specific aspect] in our relationship but feel optimistic we can sort it out. Will you be willing to meet with me about that on Thursday so I can share and we can discuss a way forward together?" Then, in the meeting, work through it this way:

1. **Desire**. The two riskiest times of a confrontation are the beginning and end. So start well by clarifying expectations. As the Harvard Negotiation Project shows in Roger Fisher and William Ury's book, *Getting to Yes,* there is more wisdom in focusing on the interests of both parties than beginning with the conclusion you have already drawn. Your job is not to talk them out of their position but to broaden the options that meet both of your interests.[9] So, after your greetings, let your first words set an atmosphere for agreement by announcing specifically what you hope to accomplish in the conversation, like: "When we walk out of this conversation, I hope you feel your interest [x] is met;" or, "I hope we both feel good about an alternative [y] that satisfies both of us;" or, "I hope you might discover that supporting me in [z] still meets your interests." You get the picture.

2. **Contrast**. Describe an outcome you don't want, and show the signs of it. For example: "However, we will both know I totally blew that intention, or we'll know something went sideways, if you leave here feeling attacked or suspicious or ambiguous, or if we pass in the hallway days later and you find yourself wondering what I feel toward you. I don't want any of that, and I think we can do better for each other today."

3. **Safety**. Make it safe by apologizing in advance for error, and invite the other person to correct you. For example: "Before I share some of my experiences with you, I value accuracy for your interests as well as mine, so I welcome you to correct any facts or misinterpretations I may have wrong."

4. **Story**. Don't begin with a summative judgment about them, but retrace the series of experiences that led to this conversation. Tell them what you saw or heard or felt or interpreted at each episode of the story. This approach conveys how a network of otherwise independent situations can be stitched together to draw some conclusions. For example, it might sounds like this: "Do you remember when [x] happened several months ago? At first, I didn't think much about it, but then [y] happened a few weeks later, and [z] again just last week. I could be misinterpreting some of this, but can you understand how I've started to notice a pattern?"

5. **Summary Judgment**. State as succinctly and insightfully as possible what all those experiences lead you to conclude. For example: "So this is what I am starting to conclude: it seems as if you take my ideas and represent them as your own to others, with no reference to me. I am happy to have a collaborative relationship, but this feels manipulative or self-serving."

6. **Listen**. Invite them to correct facts or interpretations or to tell their stories about you that have led them to their own conclusions.

7. **Active Listening**. Paraphrase what you hear. Ask clarifying questions. Affirm where you agree. Clarify where you don't and why.

8. **Action**. How you conclude the confrontation is risky if you leave things in an ambiguous place. Dialogue is helpful for understanding someone's experience, but conversation is not decision-making, and we need to leave this encounter with a clear commitment.

If you are in a position to clarify the context, do that, choosing among four options:

Is this a **command** situation, like where a parent or employer is vested with authority to decide who should be accountable for what, as changes go forward?

Is this a **consult** situation, where even one with authority invites the opinion or advocacy of another before deciding?

Is this a **vote** situation, where even if one is vested with authority, they release power to the group?

Is this a **consensus** setting, where the leader pushes for an outcome to which everyone explicitly agrees?

To illustrate, as president of a university, I rarely go into **command** mode, but I also know power is helpful if it can bring clarity and peace to chaos. For example, when two departments kept debating *ad nauseam* about who would be responsible for the ongoing content of an external digital advertising board, I just told them the debate wasn't producing a resolution, and I assigned the person who would be responsible and accountable moving forward.

Most often, however, I work from **consult** mode, retaining authority to decide but only after inviting everyone's opinions, particularly on high-stakes strategy and budgetary commitments, or in defining new accountabilities from personnel disputes.

Very rarely have I moved to a **vote**, but that fit when we were trying to decide whether to arm campus security officers with guns. After receiving research and advocacy reports, and being lobbied heavily by members of our community, I put it to a vote by the five vice presidents and myself. To maximize forthrightness and suppress hierarchy effects, I had them write their votes on paper without names. The results were 3–3! That gave me deeper insight than had I run the matter by command or consult.

Finally, even rarer still is my expectation for 100-percent **consensus**, but I do test for that with senior leaders when we name institutional priorities for the coming five-year span. Unanimity from the most senior team is important because we will all be publicly accountable on high-stakes commitments for several years.

Your Turn

We've seen how the apostle Paul suffers deeply during conflict, just like us. He adopts a biblical attitude toward conflict and follows the methodology set by Jesus to find a remedy. In this, he stewards the mystery available to us that confrontation, not avoidance, brings lasting peace.

As you lead your project and team through conflict, do not suffer what Peter Scazzero describes as the "emotional deficits" of lack of awareness of your own feelings and how others experience you. You cannot thrive in your project without a capacity to enter into others' feelings and perspective during conflict. He says success in leadership is 60 percent emotional health. Leaders can be tortured emotionally by any failure or conflict. They can get sloppy with their power and focus on outcomes alone, which is idolatrous. The signs include blaming others, shaming yourself, denial, and rationalizing. "If you have no concern that your heart might be hard or could deceive you, it already does!"[10]

Now it's your turn to practice stewarding the mystery.

- Which markers of Covey's tax or dividend of trust does your project team show? Withdrawal or angry confrontations? Evidence-gathering behaviors of others' weaknesses? Preoccupied with others' motives? Or the dividend of members honoring differences and leveraging strengths?

- With whom do you have conflict that qualifies as "crucial" (high stakes, varying opinions, strong emotions)?

- Do some self-examination. Even if you satisfy your own conscience, in what way might you possibly not be innocent (1 Cor. 4:4)? Could any hidden faults compromise the health of your confrontation (Ps. 19:12)? In an attempt to consider others above yourself before confronting (Phil. 2:3), name three admirable traits of your offender. Be honest with yourself. Do you carry worldly or godly sorrow over anything uncovered in this process (2 Cor. 7:8–13)?

- Which stage of confrontation are you in? (1) go one on one, (2) take a witness, (3) take it to the church overseers or, if relevant, a panel of trusted project colleagues, (4) shun with unconditional love to receive them back if they want to.
- Map your confrontation content (yes, literally write it out!): (1) your desire statement, (2) your contrast statement, (3) the safety statement, (4) vignettes of your story, (5) your summary judgment in one sentence, (6) listening (7) active listening (and paraphrasing what you hear from the other person), and (8) action plan (assessed by command, consult, vote, or consensus).

Confrontation is difficult, but folks with high integrity, courage, and skill reap huge benefits for themselves and their project teams who do it well. So, reader, gird your loins, and get on with it!

In the next chapter, we explore how conflict might be only one setback. Percussive hardships can leave us feeling like roadkill with vultures swirling overhead! Let's dig into the mystery that matters in responding to hardship in chapter 7.

SEVEN
PLEASED BY PAIN

This isn't me, I thought. *What's happening?* I was groomed to be un-flappable under pressure, and I mostly succeeded. But now, I had been experiencing a twitchy hand and panic attacks, for a year. The extraordinary financial pressures in my life, described in chapter 5, compounded under the radar of my consciousness.

Nearly thirty years ago, my dad piloted his twin-engine Cessna from Flint, Michigan, to North Carolina, carrying four businessmen to secure funding for the facility he would construct. En route, an engine caught fire. They crashed in a cornfield outside Columbus, Ohio. All five died. My mother learned of the crash from CNN. Attorneys later played the radio transmission of his last five minutes alive. It was all very grim.

As my young adulthood gave way to midlife, the anniversary of that event lessened in emotional intensity for the family. Where tears used to fall every November 12, humorous stories eventually took their place. Then something changed. As my own chronology ticked toward forty-nine, the age my father was when he died, the stew of my brain chemistry got spiced not only by my intense professional pressures but also by the subconscious threat of mortality. Out of the blue came a sporadic muscle twitch in my hand and cheek, sleeplessness, and then the first panic attack of my life—no surprise—while I sat on an airplane.

As soon as I took my seat on a commercial flight, a hot rush of terror swept through my chest and mind. I couldn't breathe. This was less like the slow buildup of aerobic fatigue during a jog, and more like being dunked in a swimming pool from behind and held under before you had a chance to inhale. My eyes flashed toward the exit, but panic escalated again as the center aisle clogged with onboarding guests. My path to retreat was impassable.

I speed-walked to the back of the plane, spreading out my limbs to own more personal space in the flight attendants' service station. Leaning over, with crazed eyes, I told the staff as calmly as possible, "I don't know what is happening right now. I have flown all my life, but right now I am suddenly claustrophobic and losing control."

In maternal tones, one of the attendants said, "I'm sorry, this happens frequently; if later you need pharmaceutical aid, we'll get it for you; in the meantime, would you sit for a while?" Within three minutes, the fear evaporated. I'm talking like a switch, not a slow dial. Just—gone. This both relieved and confused me.

In the weeks to come, the adversary in my brain kept haunting me. While loading a ten-seat private jet to make site visits for construction planning, it rushed me again. I bolted out and stood on the ground by the wing, my mind racing and wondering, *What is going on with me?!* I scrambled through a few face-saving scenarios if I had to cancel on this group. The pilot rounded the wing on ordinary inspections, so I whispered to him about my issue. He reassured me and brokered a compassionate deal. If, by the time we had taxied to the end of the runway, my panic still ruled, I was to give him a hand signal and we'd return to the tarmac. I didn't have to use the hand signal. Again, in just three minutes, the terror washed away.

Books taught me that this pattern can create a fear of fear—anticipating trouble before it comes. Sure enough, over the course of the next year, my fear of impending panic attacks tortured me more than the actual attacks, but still they came too: while climbing into the back of a passenger van; while sitting in a crowded church; waking in the middle of the night in a hotel room, feeling suffocated by the pitch-black darkness, where all I could do was stand against the wall, cursing my own feelings. My body and my brain were betraying me! The only way I survived hosting an Israel tour group for our organization—with its tyranny of tunnels, buses, and airplanes—was prescription medicine.

What about you? Have you suffered hardship, pain, or delay that can't be explained—whether financial, psychological, relational, health, anything? For a Christian, misery can be compounded by perceived negligence from God. Pastor and seminary professor A. J. Swoboda writes that we all eventually face "awkward Saturday." On Friday, Jesus died on the cross to save the world from sin. On Sunday, he rose from the grave, defeating the powers of evil. But nobody talks about Saturday. He lay dead for one long, endless day. If you possess the power to rise, why wait? We all have experienced Saturday in our lives, waiting nervously for an all-powerful God to rescue us from uncertainty, agony, and muddling through with no answers.[1] My wife encouraged me to confide in select board members. To my surprise, both of those I approached answered with their own stories of suffering panic attacks prompted by immense leadership pressure.

I used a self-assessment tool from Archibald Hart's *The Hidden Link between Adrenaline and Stress* that revealed my lifestyle of "hurry sickness." It classified me in "severe distress" conditions. The biological effects of adrenaline are like a rubber band stretched too wide for so long that it won't return to its original shape, even after the pressure deescalates. Stress pumps an excess of cortisol through the brain, blocking natural tranquilizers. The result, Hart explains, is "high anxiety, especially panic anxiety attacks."[2] Nutrition and exercise won't fix this. A person must learn to function at a lower level of arousal during challenge. Hardship or delay is bad enough, but especially for leaders who strive and carry the needs and hopes of others on top of our own, circumstances find and crush us. But we need not suffer silently or operate on willpower alone.

As you execute your project, hardship will come. It's time to steward a mystery that matters. God's power is sufficient to fully remedy anything, anytime, but his permissive will sometimes leaves us in unaltered pain for other kinds of benefit. God's project is that we become holy, wise, and sanctified over healthy, wealthy, and successful in the world's eyes. Pain can be an efficient path toward holiness. There is often purpose in pain. Paul keeps his wits through imprisonment, shipwreck, and public scorn, but the deeper mystery he navigates is actually becoming *pleased* with the ultimate good serviced by temporal pain. God's sustaining power arises in him even if healing power won't (Rom. 5:1–5; 2 Cor. 12:9–10). This made him, and will make us, "complete, not lacking anything" (James 1:4). My pain produced deeper empathy for others, a less idolatrous attachment to work outcomes, and (I hope) what others might experience from me as wiser counsel.

Purpose in Pain

Let there be no doubt. Paul goes *through* it! It hits the fan, and keeps doing so. How many people do you know who open their letters describing "great pressure, far beyond our ability to endure, so that we despaired of life itself" (2 Cor. 1:8), and sign off with, "remember my chains" (Col. 4:18)? Contemporaries cannot mend his trials by efficacious medicine, advanced psychology, or even a robust theology of suffering. They watch him suffer and steward spiritual mystery.

Paul compares his lifestyle to others less burdened in 2 Corinthians 11:23b–27:

> I have worked much harder, been in prison in more frequently, been flogged more severely, and been exposed to death again and again. Five times I received from the Jews the forty lashes minus one. Three times I was beaten with rods, once I was pelted with stones, three times I was shipwrecked, I spent a night and a day in the open sea, I have been constantly on the move. I have been in danger from rivers, in danger from bandits, in danger from my fellow Jews, in danger from Gentiles; in danger in the city, in danger in the country, in danger at sea; and in danger from false believers. I have labored and toiled and have often gone without sleep; I have known hunger and thirst and have often gone without food; I have been cold and naked.

Those are physical hardships. Stacked on top is something more emotional-psychological: "Besides everything else, I face daily the pressure of my concern for all the churches" (v. 28). That is tantamount to the inward pressure of an entrepreneur who knows that, if sales decline, she'll have to wreck dozens of families by layoff; or a leader of a department that is limping along with poor performance and who also aches over their sick work culture, a constant pit in the stomach from squabbles and disunity. Yes, we who lead can locate ourselves in Paul's experience, regardless of whether we've actually been shipwrecked or flogged.

Compounding the pain for a believer is the nagging question: why would a loving God allow us to suffer like that? Chad Meister, professor of philosophy at Bethel University, has so thoroughly considered the question that he published more pages than anyone in America about it. His students playfully call him Dr. Evil because he diagnoses God's allowance of evil in the lives of Christians. In *God Is Great, God Is Good*, co-edited with apologist William Lane Craig, the problem of evil is traced to Greek philosopher Epicurus in the third century BC, who claimed: "Either God wants to abolish evil and cannot, or he can but does not want to. If he wants to but cannot, he is impotent. If he can but does not want to, he is wicked. If God can abolish evil and really wants to do it, why is there evil in the world?" Yet, Meister answers, the question is decisively rebutted. "There is no logical contradiction, for it could be the case that an all-powerful and all-knowing and omnibenevolent God has good reasons to allow evil to exist and persist—perhaps, for example, for the greater good of one or more persons."[3] In short, pain can serve a purpose. This is a life-altering point.

The Jewish *New York Times* columnist David Brooks echoes this point in his book, *The Road to Character*. Pain is like standing on a weak platform. Just when life feels normal, the floor breaks loose, dropping us down into a cavity we did not know existed. Then, as we center ourselves, *boom*—that floor gives way again, collapsing us down into another cavity, and so on. Hardship forces us to descend, again and again, into the unknown territory of our inner lives, leaving us disillusioned with ourselves and with God. There are two kinds of people responding to this. One organizes their life around what Brooks calls *resumé virtues*, who value exertion to overcome obstacles. But the person who is after *eulogy virtues* is aware that pain can teach. Instead of asking, *Why me?*, the focus becomes, *What can I learn from this?* Brooks says that pain can "redeem something bad by turning it into something sacred." In this way, "it is not suffering itself that makes all the difference, but the way it is experienced."[4]

Sometimes we falsely imagine that the most public and successful leaders are endowed with talent or spiritual anointing that elevates them beyond pain. But, as mega-church preacher and bestselling author T. D. Jakes explains, people get jealous of his spectacle but don't want his hardships that come with it. The truth is, he says, "When I look back over the years and see all the hell I suffered, I would be lying to you if I told you I didn't come close to throwing in the towel on numerous occasions." As examples, he shares about how his father died when T. D. was just sixteen years old, and his family was so poor that their household utilities were shut off for lack of payment, and they survived on food stamps; in his early years his business failed, making his family so poor that his wife constructed diapers from paper towels and duct tape; later, even as his ministry grew into the national spotlight, his thirteen-year-old daughter got pregnant and his twenty-one-year-old son had a heart attack; even as his church burst at the seams, five banks denied them loans. But in all of this, he finally understood the scripture from John 15: "I am the true vine, and my Father is the gardener. He cuts off every branch in me that bears no fruit, while every branch that does bear fruit he prunes so that it will be even more fruitful" (vv. 1–2). The key for a Christian sufferer, Jakes says, is to distinguish pruning from punishment. Both types of branches face the knife, but the pain in one case frees us from an unproductive feature of our lives, while pain in the other refines and makes flourish another feature.[5] Or consider the distinction between a dagger in the hand of a bandit or a blade in the hand of a surgeon. Both inflict pain, but one's pain is for the purpose of injury while the other's is for the sake of healing. As Job says, "Though he slay me, yet I will hope in him" (13:15).

One purpose in pain, says Chaplain of the United States Senate, Barry Black, is how a man watched a beautiful butterfly trying to emerge from a cocoon. Thinking he would help as he watched the transformation taking place, he took his penknife and slit the slide of the silk cocoon. To his dismay, the butterfly flopped out, dead. What do we learn from this? God designed that butterfly to flourish from struggle. All the wiggling develops muscle that the butterfly needs to live. No skirmish, no strength.[6]

Reader, if God's primary agenda for us is holiness, wisdom, and sanctification over health, wealth, and success in the eyes of the world, then a righteous God might be pruning you when you think he punishes; he may have designed your painful circumstance for character-building struggle! This is why Paul says, despite even despairing of life: "This happened that we might not rely on ourselves but on God, who raises the dead" (2 Cor. 1:9b)—including resurrecting a dying spirit in the face of hardship. And it is why James says that the purification of pain makes us "complete, not lacking anything" (James 1:4).

God's Perfect vs. Permissive Will

Terrible frustration grows in a person who not only endures percussive hardships but also comes to believe God is "doing it" to them, like summertime kids torturing a spider on the sidewalk. We get transactional in our thinking: *if I am doing all this good for God, why does he answer with delay or pain?* In our worst moments, faith devolves and we quit on him. In other cases, faithless comrades worsen the matter. Job, for example, remains blameless during his suffering—"a man who fears God and shuns evil. And he still maintains integrity, though you [Satan] incited me against him to ruin him without any reason" (2:3)—yet his wife voices resignation instead of persistence: "Curse God and die!" (v. 9).

Clearly, we need perspective. Is what I experience God's perfect or permissive will? That is, did God produce the circumstance (punishment), or is God allowing the circumstance as an expression of our fallen, sin-sick world? It is maddening to conceive of God harming us directly, but we always have room to grow when we reflect on what we might learn from suffering. Consider Hebrews 12:4–11:

> In your struggle against sin, you have not yet resisted to the point of shedding your blood. And have you completely forgotten this word of encouragement that addresses you as a father addresses his son? It says, "My son, do not make light of the Lord's discipline, and do not lose heart when he rebukes you, because the Lord disciplines the one he

loves, and he chastens everyone he accepts as his son." Endure hardship as discipline; God is treating you as his children. For what children are not disciplined by their father? If you are not disciplined—and everyone undergoes discipline—then you are not legitimate, not true sons and daughters at all. Moreover, we have all had human fathers who disciplined us and we respected them for it. How much more should we submit to the Father of spirits and live! They disciplined us for a little while as they thought best; but God disciplines us for our good, in order that we may share in his holiness. No discipline seems pleasant at the time, but painful. Later on, however, it produces a harvest of righteousness and peace for those who have been trained by it.

These aren't flowery platitudes. Paul endures a "thorn in the flesh" (2 Cor. 12:7), his metaphor for an irritant in his life that God has either produced or permitted, without relief. As Jon Bloom says, "The fact that we really don't know what Paul's thorn was turns out to be both merciful and instructive to us."[7] On one hand, its ambiguous identity allows us all to identify with Paul from whatever our own afflictions might be, whether physical, psychological, relational, financial, spiritual, or whatever. And on the other hand, it's instructive because the thorn is less the point than God's purpose in it.

Paul comes to understand his thorn as the portal for God's sustaining power, if he can't experience God's remedying power. "Because of these surpassingly great revelations" that have been granted to Paul, God has kept Paul "from becoming conceited" by giving him the thorn in his flesh, "a messenger of Satan, to torment me. Three times I pleaded with the Lord to take it away from me. But he said to me, 'My grace is sufficient for you, for my power is made perfect in weakness'" (2 Cor. 12:7–9a). Okay. I get that. Pain keeps us humble. But here is the mystery that matters: "Therefore I will boast all the more gladly about my weaknesses"—the actual word Paul uses in Greek for "boast" is *kauchesomai*, or, "I will be proud of this pain." What?! Why?—"so that Christ's power may rest on me" (v. 9b). That is endurance power—for Christ to fulfill his purpose despite years of scorn, lies, and abuse. "That is why, for Christ's sake, I delight in weaknesses, in insults, in hardships, in persecutions, in difficulties. For when I am weak, then I am strong" (v. 10).

Paul's Greek word for "delight" is *eudoko*, or "to be pleased with its purpose." To capture this meaning more deeply, Paul uses the same word in Romans 15:26 to explain how Christians are delighted with—or pleased with the purpose of—their financial donations to the poor in Jerusalem. So in the same way one feels pleasure in the purpose of financial sacrifice to meet needs of the poor, we can also be pleased to know our hardships are a portal for a donation of power from the Holy Spirit, to endure. This perspective makes it possible for Paul to say in another place, "We are hard pressed on every side, but not crushed; perplexed, but not in despair; persecuted, but not abandoned; struck down, but not destroyed. . . . Therefore we do not lose heart. Though outwardly we are wasting away, yet inwardly we are being renewed day by day" (2 Cor. 4:8–9, 16). God is teleological. He has purpose and will bring all things into that purpose, to his intended end. But, though he remains sovereign over all things, he allows human agency.

Does this work, you know, in real life?! Ask my mother, who—despite living a blessed life—parented three young boys through incurable heart arrhythmia, which sent her into cardiac arrest three times. On one occasion my father huddled his sons, whispering, "She may not come home this time." Despite prayer, tithing, and showing mercy toward others it was frustrating to receive no remedy—until.

Five years later, while on a Northern Michigan retreat, she was terrorized to discover, while out for a long walk, that she had forgotten to take her thrice-daily life-saving medication. Always, previously, failure to take the medicine would send her into arrhythmia. But that day, she was fine. Then another day, the same. Upon returning home, she went to see her cardiologist, who said there was no medical explanation but that her examination appeared as if she had never had the condition at all. She was completely healed.

How can we understand this theologically other than, indeed, God permitted her thorn to work perseverance, character, and hope in her to depths she never could have otherwise known, and he constructed a platform of influence for her to testify about this miracle through publications and preaching to the encouragement of thousands whose miracles might still come.

Or look to a change of spirit even if the body is not restored. Thomas Gilovich and Lee Ross tell in their book about how Mark Zupan and his soccer teammates for Florida Atlantic University went out drinking in October 1993. As Mark grew drunk, he found his way to the bed of a friend's truck to sleep it off. The owner of the truck—Mark's friend, Chris Igoe—drove off, unaware Mark was in the back. Chris's inebriation blurred his vision, he lost control of the vehicle on the highway, and the truck slammed into a fence. The collision threw Mark into a drainage canal, severing his spine and leaving him with quadriplegia. Remarkably, Mark's perspective was, "In truth, my accident has been the best thing that could have ever happened to me. I'm not trying to be glib. What I am saying is that it has been the single most defining event of my life, and without it I wouldn't have done the things I've done and met so many incredible people. I wouldn't have come to understand my friends and family the way I do, and feel the kind of love they have for me, and I for them."[8]

While most able-bodied people say they would rather die than become quadriplegic, research shows that 86 percent of paralyzed patients view their quality of life as average to above average. Yet fewer than one in five doctors who attend to those patients believe their own lives could be as satisfying if *they* suffered such injuries.

Mark experienced what we all can. There is something deeper than moment-to-moment pleasure. It is what philosophers call *eudaimonia*, or a broad sense of well-being that comes from feeling that one's life is worthwhile, meaningful, and well lived. Disability is not identity. People with disabilities are also parents who enjoy their children, foodies who love to taste and experiment in the kitchen or at restaurants, creatives who express themselves—just as much as those who are not disabled. Well-being can eclipse pain—if we let it.

Pain Confirms, Rather Than Contradicts, Your Calling

Contrary to popular assumption, God does sometimes send his loved ones into trouble, and for good reason. Paul reveals as much in Acts 20:22–23: the Spirit compels him to work in Jerusalem, and while he does not know what awaits him there, he says, "I only know that in every city the Holy

Spirit warns me that prison and hardships are facing me." But if God loves us, why would God do that?!

In chapter 4, we discussed how calling is the dawning awareness that we aren't made by God for *everything*, but that we are definitely made for *something*. This truth echoes through many scriptures (Acts 17:26; Eph. 2:10; Phil. 3:12; 2 Thess. 1:11). Calling awakens a desire to be responsible for something, even if others show little interest in it. That can be isolating and burdensome. As you enter that project, you feel partly constituted for it (in your talent and experience), but a spiritual calling always requires a certain amount of courage as well. A project we can execute under naturally accessed resources (people, funds, support systems) is called a plan; what we name "calling" is by its nature bigger and beyond our resources, requiring supernatural intervention. In this way, God gets all the glory as things work out. Think of it like this. You are like a sponge. God fills you with ability for an assignment that will squeeze you with trouble, but what God put in you leaks out all over the situation like healing salve. In this way, hardship confirms your calling, rather than contradicts it. Especially for leaders so heavily burdened by their responsibilities, persistence in the face of difficulty is a faithful "response" to God's "ability": responsibility.

Once you are committed to your calling, waiting for God's intervention need not rely on willpower alone! Alan Kreider explains that in 250 AD, when our ancestors in the faith were imprisoned, to be martyred for public entertainment, there was simultaneously an epidemic raging through northern Africa that killed a million people. Archaeological records show that luminaries like Origen, Tertullian, and Cyprian extolled patience as the triumphant Christian virtue, with Origen emphasizing Paul's words to the Romans: "Not only so, but we also glory in our sufferings, because we know that suffering produces perseverance; perseverance, character; and character, hope. And hope does not put us to shame, because God's love has been poured out into our hearts through the Holy Spirit, who has been given to us" (5:3–5).[9]

Paul's Greek word to explain what God does in us as we wait on perseverance, character, and hope is *katergazetai*, which carries a sense that God is fashioning a substance within us, something approximating fermentation.

When you observe wine, kombucha, yogurt, bread, or any other substance that undergoes fermentation, absolutely nothing on the outside appears to change, but inwardly a chemical reaction fundamentally changes its nature. So too with us! Even if our circumstances have not changed, God ferments traits inside us that did not exist before our suffering, or at least to the depth they now register.

Further, we can gain perspective on God sending us into trouble by learning from what Robert Morgan calls the *Red Sea Rules*, a study of the Israelites during the exodus. God's people had been enslaved for four hundred years, but Moses leads them out. They are thrilled with their freedom until they encounter a harsh reality: God has deliberately led them into an impossible situation, putting them between a sea that is too deep to cross ahead and a fierce army bent on their destruction behind. They are cornered, like rabbits encircled by wolves. But, Morgan says, "The same God who led you in will lead you out!"[10]

Just a few lessons from their dilemma: God means for you to be where you are. Your circumstances are not a mistake. If God is sovereign, we are never victims of circumstance. In the midst of hardship, don't ask the wrong question. Instead of, "How quickly can I get out of this mess?" consider, "How could God be glorified in this situation?" In fact, the exodus dilemma is orchestrated to demonstrate God's power so following generations might trust him. This is like Jesus healing the blind man in John 9. People ask, "Is he blind due to sin?" but Jesus says, "No, this happened so God's power might be revealed in him." Similarly, why does Jesus wait a few days before raising Lazarus from the dead? It foreshadows his own three days in the tomb before resurrection. There is a lesson in the waiting period! Morgan says, "Sometimes plodding is better than plotting!"[11]

Your Turn

As you execute on your project, bank on it: hardship will come. Keep your head when the heart melts under its pressure. This chapter intends to equip you for that eventuality. As Paul reminds the Christians who are persecuted by Roman authorities, "For everything that was written in the past was written to teach us, so that through the endurance taught in the Scriptures and the encouragement they provide we might have hope" (Rom. 15:4).

These seven tests can help you assess how well you are stewarding the mystery of being pleased by the purpose in your pain, holding out hope during hardship:

1. If the object of your hope can be secured on your own, we call that a plan, not hope. Plans are good, but Christian hope is daring and relies on the supernatural intervention of God.

   Question: Over the past few months, have you discussed with someone a God-sized development for your life that is clearly beyond your own ability to produce? If yes, you have daring hope. If no, start. You have one life to live. Go for it.

2. Christian hope believes God has sufficient power to redeem any situation, anytime. If finances are punching you in the gut, or a relationship is straining your peace, or a health challenge bogs you down, in these we remember his power.

   Question: Consider the particularly tough issue in your life, the really perplexing or maddening one. Though it burdens you, do you believe God can redeem it at any given moment—even tomorrow? If yes, you have daring hope. If no, make a study of scriptures where God came through, in order to bolster your faith.

3. Christian hope believes God is at work for our good (Rom. 8:28), even if his activity is outside our awareness. It is similar to knowing that, while you observe a frozen lake, fish still live and move underneath. There is activity in God we cannot see.

   Question: Think of that area of your life where God has been silent. Do you believe he is ahead of you, arranging things in advance? If so, you have daring hope.

4. Christian hope is relaxed about the future, confident in whatever may come. A hopeful person is at peace. Their confidence in God quiets their worry. We remember the woman of noble character in

Proverbs 31 who "can laugh at the days to come" (v. 25) because she knows confidently that God is sovereign.

Question: Are you relaxed about the future? If so, you have daring hope.

5. Christian hope is oriented as much toward inner character as external outcomes. As Eric Metaxas records in his biography about Dietrich Bonhoeffer, Dietrich wrote to his fiancée, Maria, during his stay in an eight-foot-by-five-foot cell in a Gestapo prison in Nazi Germany, "Pain is a holy angel who shows treasures to men which otherwise remain hidden. Through pain men become greater than through all the joys in the world."[12]

Question: Do you hunt for character and maturity during your hardship as much as release from difficulty? If so, you have daring hope.

6. Christian hope is both individual and corporate, and it reaches across time. You might hope that your own circumstance can be redeemed, but what about the needs of your family, church, business, or city? God can interrupt even the thickest legacy of dysfunction, corruption, or failure bequeathed to you, but more—he can restore an era of peace and favor for your children and grandchildren to come.

Question: Do you believe God can redeem a situation facing your family, city, or nation? If so, you have daring hope.

7. Christian hope is so close to imagination that we can hardly tell the difference. Michael Wear says in his book about his work in the Obama administration, "Authentic hope only arrives once our other hopes—whether personal or social—are found insufficient or false."[13] I think imagination for hope shrinks because, during struggle, we curate sour memories of disappointment like ugly art in our souls. After a while, behind our eyes rests a dim resignation that God will never surprise us or transcend our circumstance. In this, bad memory overtakes imagination. But there are others who, despite disappointment, manage their memories to focus on God's faithfulness to others or

themselves. That focus fuels imagination for how God might work again. In this we anticipate God's presence, not absence. Hope rises!

Question: Even in the midst of your most difficult challenge, if you daydream out your window, does your imagination produce scenarios and developments for how God might miraculously rescue you? If so, you have daring hope.

If on any of these factors you don't yet align, now you have something to pray about, search Scripture over, and seek counsel from mature believers.

You're ready for a final turn toward the ultimate mystery to steward: bearing witness as you go. Flip the page and let's get on it.

EIGHT
BEAR WITNESS TO CHRIST AS YOU GO

A vivid opportunity dropped into my lap. Call it a holy appointment. During a break from my work in Korea, we took the kids for a half-week tour of Beijing. It was fantastic: climbing the Great Wall, observing tai chi in the large public squares, and visiting a tea-manufacturing plant. Best of all was the Forbidden City, the largest palace in the world—protected by a moat and twenty-five-foot wall—to house and honor the godlike stature of five centuries of emperors.

Our guide, a young Chinese woman, was kind and hospitable as she led us over the course of four days. There was plenty of time for personal dialogue between sites. We learned that, while modern China officially has no religion, half the population claims atheism. Hundreds of millions others, including our guide, still feel the influence of that nation's deep history with Buddhism, Taoism, and pantheistic religion. Our moment arrived as we wandered through the Temple of Heaven, a six-hundred-year-old house of worship, the world's longest-surviving structure for sacrificial offerings to appease the gods of harvest. With no one grabbing our guide's attention, my wife and I invited her to stand with us by that altar. She already knew of our faith, so we applied it.

"Imagine," we said, "that the sacrifice of sheep or oxen does not appease the gods on this altar and the harvest is lost. Though the emperor would be desperate to meet the needs of his people, it would seem too great a sacrifice to place his own son on that altar—a young boy who hadn't done anything wrong. But that's exactly what God did for us, making Jesus the supreme sacrifice and final penalty for all sin. Only, it's deeper—because Jesus volunteered. He went to that cross willingly, with you on his mind." Her face fell in humility as she nodded with understanding. In our holy huddle, the true God entered her heart by prayer of repentance and gratitude to Jesus. We gave her a Bible, and then we never saw her again. Maybe a corner of heaven will be crowded with Chinese Christians because of her influence.

God still saves today in every nation, and if you train your eyes to see as God does, souls will seek this solace in your network of relationships. Here is your chance to steward this ultimate mystery of God—the salvation of souls. My sense is that the times are ripe, even in work settings. American business has entered a new paradigm that is less about profit and more about the social fabric of the community. So says Josh Bersin in a research project conducted by the national consulting firm Deloitte. Today, 7 in 10 corporate leaders name the growth of their partners and region as important as market share; 8 in 10 make citizenship essential; employee well-being and longevity are vital. Though project leaders are not elected like politicians to represent the interests of their community, today their boards, employees, and customers expect more 360-degree thinking about the common good. In fact, Bersin reports that 40 percent of consumers are more likely to buy from companies whose CEOs have gone public on social positions they value.[1]

In 2021, JP Morgan Chase CEO Jamie Dimon made headlines for his public statements in support of voter rights in the American South. Why would a banker do that? Because his clients increasingly expect leaders to demonstrate an interest in and care for the whole person, not only their bank accounts. As you manage your own project, don't get so task-oriented that you miss this prompt for whole-life considerations. That team member or customer across the room isn't a cog in an economic wheel but a walking soul, pondering the quality of work life more than ever, along with work-home balance, and as longer lifespans create sixty-year careers their life satisfaction can trump wages. In fact, pollster John Zogby found, after asking Americans for decades about the "American dream," that now only half say it requires material success, the rest favoring spiritual fulfillment over commercialism. And the groups most likely to advocate spiritual goals over accumulating stuff aren't old, wealthy folks already drowning in their possessions. The group most likely to advocate this mindset are parents under forty who earn less than $50,000 a year.[2]

And, contrary to cultural folklore that next-generation leaders are spiritually adrift, John Schmalzbauer and Kathleen Mahoney say that college is no longer a secularizing influence, as it was for Baby Boomers. The generations following the Boomers experienced an increased likelihood of affiliating with a religious group while in college. Also, UCLA's Alexander Astin surveyed 112,000 American college students over a decade and found that half of freshmen wanted their schools to "encourage their personal expression of spirituality."[3]

Enter, the gospel. This book probes several mysteries that matter, but here is an open door in our culture to participate more assertively in the ultimate mystery—the salvation of souls through personal evangelism. Paul tells the church in Rome that the riddle about the Messiah is solved: "Now to him who is able to establish in accordance with my gospel, the message I proclaim about Jesus Christ, in keeping with the revelation of the mystery hidden for long ages past, but now revealed and made known through the prophetic writings by the command of the eternal God, so that all . . . might come to the obedience that comes from faith" (Rom. 16:25–26).

So, reader, get ready. Be watchful and vigilant. The Scriptures tap you on the shoulder: "But in your hearts revere Christ as Lord. Always be prepared to give an answer to everyone who asks you to give the reason for the hope that you have" (1 Pet. 3:15). That is, bear witness as you go through the ordinary rhythms of life. Whether at work, home, school, volunteering in your community, or running errands, bear witness to your encounters with Christ as you go. Motivating us is the love of Christ, as Paul tells the church in Corinth: "Since, then, we know what it is to fear the Lord, we try to persuade others. . . . For Christ's love compels us, because we are convinced that one died for all, and therefore all died. And he died for all, that those who live should no longer live for themselves but for him who died for them and was raised again. So from now on we regard no one from a worldly point of view" (2 Cor. 5:11a, 14–16a). Yes, walking and talking souls surround us. Waiting.

How Paul Preaches the Mystery

A fundamental fact in bearing witness as we go is the prevenient grace of God. The real headline is not that we seek God but that God seeks us, constantly and creatively. "No one can come to me [Jesus] unless the Father who sent me draws them, and I will raise them up at the last day" (John 6:44). And "when he [the Holy Spirit] comes, he will prove the world to be in the wrong about sin and righteousness and judgment" (John 16:8). The Spirit opens our minds to understand the Scriptures (see Luke 24:45). We should not be surprised by seekers, for everyone wonders if there is more to this life and the one to come. "[God] has made everything beautiful in its time. He has also set eternity in the human heart; yet no one can fathom what God has done from beginning to end" (Eccl. 3:11).

Meanwhile, we are to focus on seekers, not rejecters. Jesus instructs the disciples, "Whatever town or village you enter, search there for some worthy person and stay at their house until you leave. As you enter the home, give it your greeting. If the home is deserving, let your peace rest on it; if it is not, let your peace return to you. If anyone will not welcome you or listen to your words, leave that home or town and shake the dust off your feet" (Matt. 10:11–14). Shaking the dust off one's feet is a symbolic gesture indicating that we are not to waste time with those who are not interested in the gospel.

The ultimate mystery Paul stewards is preaching the gospel—a good-news message that "through Jesus the forgiveness of sins is proclaimed to you. Through him everyone who believes is set free from every sin, a justification you were not able to obtain under the law of Moses" (Acts 13:38b–39). This is a salvation by faith, not works (Eph. 2:8–9). And what is faith? Simply trusting in a promise on the credibility of the Promiser. You have faith in physicians, mechanics, and bridge engineers. So, too, trust in the promise of salvation because of who is credible to offer it.

Paul sketches out the sin problem and grace solution. Sincere people debate what actually constitutes sin. It is at minimum a condition into which we are all born, that inward default toward selfishness and feeding the desires of this material world. In this, "all have sinned and fall short of the glory of God" (Rom. 3:23), "the wages of sin is death" (Rom. 6:23a), and this must be atoned for because "without holiness no one will see the Lord" (Heb. 12:14b). Jesus became the supreme sacrifice. Our faith in his act and divinity erases the curse of sin from our lives, giving us peace with God in this life and the one to come.

Sin is also an action. Galatians 5:19–21 tells us: "The acts of the flesh are obvious: sexual immorality, impurity and debauchery; idolatry and witchcraft; hatred, discord, jealousy, fits of rage, selfish ambition, dissensions, factions and envy; drunkenness, orgies, and the like. I warn you, as I did before, that those who live like this will not inherit the kingdom of God." We also sin by conscious inaction, as James says: "If anyone, then, knows the good they ought to do and doesn't do it, it is sin for them" (4:17).

The good news, therefore, is that the grace and mercy of God await. Writing to the church in Ephesus, Paul says,

> As for you, you were dead in your transgressions and sins, in which you used to live when you followed the ways of this world and of the ruler of the kingdom of the air, the spirit who is now at work in those who are disobedient. All of us also lived among them at one time, gratifying the cravings of our flesh and following its desires and thoughts. Like the rest, we were by nature deserving of wrath. But because of his great love for us, God, who is rich in mercy, made us alive with Christ even when we were dead in transgressions—it is by grace you have been saved. (2:1–5)

Salvation requires belief and profession: "For it is with your heart that you believe and are justified, and it is with your mouth that you profess your faith and are saved" (Rom. 10:10).

Also, while our approach to understanding this salvation benefits from support, no negotiator or moderator is necessary. As Paul charges his protégé, Timothy, God "wants all people to be saved and to come to a knowledge of the truth. For there is one God and mediator between God and mankind, the man Christ Jesus, who gave himself as a ransom for all people" (1 Tim. 2:4–6a). We don't need a priest, pastor, or another believer before Christ will receive us!

After we repent of sin and enjoy righteousness by faith in the work of Christ to erase the penalty of sin, what is the impact of sin going forward? Sincere people draw different conclusions from Scripture about that. For one branch of the faith, we cannot live above sin, so when God looks at a Christian he sees Christ's covering over sin, a gifted righteousness. In this, the Christian person is not changed, only God's response to sin in that person. What remains is a sinning religion. However, if sin is a conscious, willful act, we can be freed from sin, no longer slavishly serving its desires but becoming slavish instead to righteousness (Rom. 6:15–18). Richard Taylor explains:

> Notice how confusing and self-contradictory it is to tell the sinner to repent, to act, as though he were partially responsible for his own salvation, then tell him that, once saved, he is eternally secure. It implies that [humanity] has responsibility before conversion but none after. It means that a person has ability to get into the kingdom but none to get out. It gives sinners a free moral agency, but denies it to Christians. A strange dilemma! Surely if a sinner is morally responsible to become saved he is just as morally responsible to remain saved. It is absurd to infer that conversion destroys freedom of the will, or marks the end of probation.[4]

Therefore, a Spirit-filled person proceeds in the fruit of the Spirit: "But the fruit of the Spirit is love, joy, peace, forbearance, kindness, goodness, faithfulness, gentleness and self-control. Against such things there is no law. Those who belong to Christ Jesus have crucified the flesh with its passions and desires. Since we live by the Spirit, let us keep in step with the Spirit" (Gal. 5:22–25).

Now We Preach the Mystery: From Proclamation to Discipleship

As noted in chapter 1, although Paul was a figure of historic necessity and special gifting for missions, we relate to God just as Paul did—as those who have never materially met Jesus and must cultivate a competence for walking in the Spirit. Just as the Father sent the Son, the Sprit followed the Son, and the Trinity operates in Paul's life, we too are sent by God to preach the gospel, regardless of our profession, credentials, or titling.

While spiritual gifts might allocate unusual effectiveness to persons to prophesy (speak to others for their encouragement) or to teach (explaining the gospel to those already converted), we are together "a chosen people, a royal priesthood, a holy nation, God's special possession, that you may declare the praises of him who called you out of darkness into his wonderful light. Once you were not a people, but now you are the people of God; once you had not received mercy, but now you have received mercy" (1 Peter 2:9–10). Art Lindsley explains that all Christians should regard themselves as functioning priests without the professional designation. Martin Luther was so convinced of this doctrine that he taught that "this word priest should become as common as the word Christian."[5]

The Old Testament anticipated this era when God said through Moses on Mount Sinai, "You will be for me a kingdom of priests and a holy nation" (Exod. 19:6a). Isaiah prophesied a time when "you will be called priests of the LORD" (61:6). Because Christ is the highest priest, and we are now in him, all Christians take membership in that royal priesthood, to proclaim his message. We no longer offer ceremonial sacrifices of bulls or sheep, but we retain the moral mission with "spiritual sacrifices acceptable to God through Jesus Christ" (1 Pet. 2:5b)—things like prayer, praise, repentance, kindness, and more.

Actually, there is a spiritual mystery at work here—the mere profession of our faith, unimpressive as it might feel, can awaken faith in others because "faith comes from hearing the message, and the message is heard through the word about Christ" (Rom. 10:17). Indeed, this is a mystery—that "God was pleased through the foolishness of what was preached to save those who believe" (1 Cor. 1:21b). We all, then, serve as "Christ's ambassadors, as though God were making his appeal through us" (2 Cor. 5:20a).

We ought not be intimidated by this. To bear witness does not require formulas or eloquence. In fact, Paul admits to this very fact in 1 Corinthians 2:1–5:

> And so it was with me, brothers and sisters. When I came to you, I did not come with eloquence or human wisdom as I proclaimed to you the testimony about God. For I resolved to know nothing while I was with you except Jesus Christ and him crucified. I came to you in weakness

with great fear and trembling. My message and my preaching were not with wise and persuasive words, but with a demonstration of the Spirit's power, so that your faith might not rest on human wisdom, but on God's power.

To bear witness as you go assumes you anticipate witnessing opportunities, to testify what God has done for you, without carrying the weight of persuasiveness or doctrinal infallibility.

In preparing what to say, James K. A. Smith explains that we should not think of Christianity as *knowledge*. "It's not that we start with beliefs and doctrine and then come up worship practices that properly 'express' these (cognitive) beliefs; rather, we begin with worship, and articulated beliefs bubble up from there."[6] Our encounter with and response to Christ is the salvation, with doctrine explaining it later. Remember how the Pharisees, guardians of doctrine, investigate Jesus by interrogating a healed blind man? When they press this guy to explain who Jesus is, he answers, "Whether he is a sinner or not, I don't know. One thing I do know. I was blind but now I see!" (John 9:25). That is a testimony every person can give.

If you are to bear witness as you go, it will help to organize how you will maximize your influence beyond proclaiming Christ and into longer-term discipling relationships. Robert Coleman offers a set of controlling principles in Jesus's method that can be extrapolated for our lives:

1. **Selection**. People, not programs, are God's method, including his frequent use of unlearned carriers of the gospel message (see Acts 4:13). Jesus also focuses on just a few key relationships, rather than the masses. He begins with a dozen disciples but spends the most time with only three. Only Peter, James, and John are invited into the sick room of Jairus's daughter (Mark 5:37); travel with Jesus to the Mount of Transfiguration (Mark 9:2); and pray separately with him in the garden of Gethsemane (Mark 14:33).

2. **Association**. Unstructured relationship time—just sharing life together—is the primary context for discipleship. For example, as Jesus's popularity grows, he increasingly spends private time with his group on retreats and trips. Private follow-ups after group gatherings are strategic for him, such as visiting Zacchaeus (Luke 19:7); wel-

coming Bartimaeus (Mark 10:52); and lingering for two days after ministering to the Samaritan woman at the well (John 4:40).

3. **Consecration**. Those willing to be discipled need not be smart, only loyal. For example, Jesus does not scramble after deserters, begging to retain them (John 6:60–70). The premise of our discipling relationships is to work with the committed: "No one who puts a hand to the plow and looks back is fit for service in the kingdom of God" (Luke 9:62); "Whoever wants to be my disciple must deny themselves and take up their cross and follow me. For whoever wants to save their life will lose it, but whoever loses their life for me will find it" (Matt. 16:24–25).

4. **Impartation**. Just as Jesus shares everything he has received from the Father, we must remain close enough—by prayer, Scripture, and fellowship—to share what *we* receive from God. One cannot give what one does not possess. Jesus makes it clear that evangelism is mediated through the Holy Spirit, who gives us the words to speak (Matt. 10:19–20).

5. **Demonstration**. Put plainly, Jesus tells his disciples, "I have set you an example that you should do as I have done for you" (John 13:15). He also models prayer (see Luke 11:1–4). More than ninety times, he cites or alludes to Old Testament truths. He teaches creatively, elaborating when they don't understand (see Mark 4:1–20). We can too.

6. **Delegation**. We should assign discipleship duties to those within our network. Jesus empowers his disciples to baptize people and minister in pairs (Mark 6:7; Luke 10:1); he also defines the scope of their work (Matt. 10:8) and liberates them from wasting time on skeptics (Matt. 10:11–14).

7. **Supervision**. He debriefs after ministry experiences (Mark 6:30; Luke 10:17) and provides clarifying teachings. For example, Jesus separates from the disciples for a time, then in reunion learns that, despite their spiritual authority, an afflicted boy has not been helped. Jesus heals the boy himself, then teaches the group about why they weren't able to do it on their own (see Mark 9:14–29).

8. **Reproduction**. After we disciple others into maturity, they should be challenged to disciple others. In this way, the kingdom of God grows like a tiny mustard seed that becomes a tree greater than all others (see Matt. 13:31–32). However, Jesus does not expect everyone to whom we bear witness to come to salvation. Narrow is the road to salvation and broad the path to destruction (see Matt. 7:13–14); not all who call themselves Christians will be saved, only doers of the truth (see Matt. 7:21). It all comes down to this: as we confess Christ as Messiah, God builds the church and harvests a good crop (see Matt. 16:18; 1 Cor. 3:6–11). Through our word of testimony, others will believe in him (John 17:20).[7]

There is one more mystery in this. We gain insight into our own salvation in the process of bearing witness. Paul explains to the slave-owner and new convert Philemon that he should show Onesimus, his slave, godly grace. Their relationship is no longer merely hierarchical; they are also brothers in the Lord. This insight will come as he shares his faith, for Paul writes, "I pray that your partnership with us in the faith may be effective in deepening your understanding of every good thing we share for the sake of Christ" (Philemon 1:6). Reader, it's the same for you—really! Bear witness, disciple, and rediscover to new depths all that Christ has done for you.

Revival through You—Yes, You

Now, what happens if bearing witness grows beyond individual efforts into a movement? Sometimes, in some places, a catalytic thing occurs. People often call it spiritual renewal or revival. This sounds like something that happens elsewhere, rumored church-speak of mythological proportions, believed for others yet rarely experienced at home. But we can demystify it. Elmer Towns and Doug Porter analyzed patterns across many broad-based encounters with God in *The Ten Greatest Revivals Ever*. Whether it was the 1904 explosion from Azusa Street, the Great Awakenings, the Laymen's Prayer Revival of New York, or others, revival is simply this: "an extraordinary work of God marked by repentance of sin, an intense awareness of God's presence, renewal of obedience, and a deepened corporate zeal to win souls for Christ."[8] Awareness of God, obedience to him, and zeal should probably characterize an ordinary Christian year! But occasionally, the adjectives are real—an extraordinary work of God, intense awareness, deepened zeal. We are not calling for an inducement of emotional consciousness toward these aspects of spiritual life. We can sometimes bully folks to "get broken," or invite them to a charged worship service to "get wrecked." But you're not spiritually malfunctioning or insincere if you lack emotion. The point is that we should minimize outcome measures of emotion while still validating special outpourings of God that are often called revival.

I want to normalize this with examples. Notably, though church leaders always emerge in revivals, no significant preachers have marked these movements. Instead, prayer has. Jeremiah Lanphier began a noon prayer meeting for business people, disciplined for just sixty minutes, on Fulton Street in New York City in 1857, under the agitation of political unrest, imminent civil war, and a financial panic where banks failed, railroads bankrupted and factories closed. The format was simple: one song, a five-minute testimony, then just—pray. At the first prayer meeting, only six showed up. But within months, the crowd filled three rooms, and at year's end, front-page stories reported six thousand participants each week, with another six thousand in Pittsburgh. Various businesses posted signs at noon that said, "Will reopen after prayer meeting." This hunger for and practice of prayer spread across the nation.[9]

H. J. Heinz felt conviction in his Chicago prayer group, saying, "I want to be known as a Sunday school man, not a catsup man."[10] John Wannamaker, owner of the department store by his name in Philadelphia and later U.S. Postmaster, also joined a prayer group and became superintendent of the largest Sunday school in America at Immanuel Church with three thousand participants. A Methodist physician, Walter Palmer, and his wife, Phoebe—who became a famous evangelist in her own right—led a camp meeting on a farm in Ontario, Canada, where five hundred were converted. In following days, at a camp near Toronto, twenty thousand people attended weekend services.

This impact reached across geography, denominations, and age groups. Reader, should you be young, don't discount your influence. In fact, Towns and Porter observe a pattern. "The case throughout history is, when revival came, it was first noticed among the youth," such as the Asbury College revival of 1970, which spilled out to 130 other campuses, the Jesus Movement of 1965, the Calvary Chapel movement, and Independent Baptist Sunday school revival.[11] As Paul reminds Timothy, "Don't let anyone look down on you because you are young, but set an example for the believers in speech, in conduct, in love, in faith, and in purity" (1 Tim. 4:12).

Further, Towns and Porter explain that, as long as participants meet conditions laid out in 2 Chronicles 7:14 (corporate and individual humility, prayer, repentance), history shows that: (1) revival is not limited by denominational allegiances or doctrinal positions; (2) while people often express fervency during revival, the testimony of history is that there are not often sensationalistic features (running in the aisles, fainting); (3) revival comes during crisis and peaceful times; and, among others, (4) some movements are localized to a church or city, while others spread across regions or nations.[12]

Can you now see your place in revival need not be rare or fantastical? God has already put in you what is needed to bear witness as you go— namely, an experience with God and a testimony about that, without having to carry the burden of doctrinal mastery. The church belongs to Jesus, not you. It is the Holy Spirit's job, not yours, to seek, find, convict, convert, and mature. Your role is to watch for opportunities, be a friend, listen well, share honestly, and pray. Ask the Holy Spirit to do his work through you, and then, as my childhood pastor used to say, "Let the loose ends drag!"

Your Turn

Let's prepare to bear witness. Apply the principles from Coleman's master plan of evangelism.

1. Selection: Who are two people already in your relational network who appear to be open to the message of Christ?
2. Association: How might you take advantage of a retreat or activity, anything that offers a big block of unstructured time to spend with those two folks, in order to probe their spiritual status?
3. Consecration: Do those individuals show potential or intent to seek more fervently, to devote themselves to an encounter with God? If not, keep looking for other folks in your network.

4. Impartation: Is your testimony only about long-ago encounters with the Spirit? What discipleship disciplines do you already practice, or would you commit to, to stay fresh in your relationship with Christ, so you have something current to share with others?

5. Demonstration: With those one or two people in mind, have you shown them how to pray, how to search Scripture, how to worship? If not, what is an upcoming opportunity to bring them into fellowship with you and others who are already mature in the faith and capable of modeling?

6. Delegation: If these few under your influence have accepted Christ and are growing in knowledge of him, in what ways could you invite them to carry the discipleship load with you, for the benefit of others?

7. Supervision: A good model for discipleship can be this—you act while they watch, then they act with you, then you watch while they act, and then provide feedback.

8. Reproduction: When your people appear ready, encourage them to replicate your relationship pattern with seekers in their network. Continue to encourage and coach as they bear witness while they go.

If you lean in on this, get ready! I'm telling you, you are living in one of the most answerable prayers possible by God. People and their eternal need will arrive in your life faster than you can spell S-A-V-E-D. But God is the solution, not you. He'll guide you so you can guide them. It's fun! Enjoy it.

CONCLUSION

The central claim of this book has been that there is remarkable guidance during what appears to be mundane experience. Don't neglect spiritual power as you execute prototypical phases of your workplace, home, or community projects. This power is as real as the internet connection or radio signals flying over your head right now. Though the Holy Spirit is invisible, you can access him if you have the right frequency.

The exciting reality is that we are not simply forgiven of sin but are also transformed into people who "walk by the Spirit" (Gal. 5:16) and enjoy a God-given competence for everyday discernment (2 Cor. 3:5). Indeed, you can be just like Paul, a steward of the mysteries of God (1 Cor. 4:1). I challenge you to assume an identity as an SMG. This is both who you are and what you do, to powerful effect. A change of identity will affect your sight and insight, attitude and behavior, and certainly your expectations for living a life normalized with God's guidance.

These chapters demonstrate especially operative spiritual mysteries, as you watch for signs of change, operate in the timing of God, receive accomplices you didn't recruit, are rewarded for financial stewardship, healthfully confront during conflict for lasting peace, are pleased by the purpose of your pain, and bear witness as you go. The ultimate mystery is that Jesus saves!

I leave you with this: Saudi Arabia's Rub' Al-Khali ("Empty Quarter") Desert was one of the last unconquered frontiers on Earth, 200 miles from anything, a land of towering sand dunes and immense salt flats, with temperatures exceeding 120 degrees. But some saw more than sand. They believed there was oil under the wasteland. A company, Saudi Aramco, did their due diligence. Without total proof, it was decision time. They committed—under the hope of their belief—funding and planning for the construction of a 240-mile access road into that desert, with a 400-mile pipeline and a small city of outbuildings and residences for large teams of workers. But as construction launched, a problem emerged. They needed sand. The fine grains of the desert were unsuitable for use in making concrete. So they did the unthinkable. They brought more sand into the desert, by the truckload. Just like all good stories, their risk paid off, handsomely! The result was unprecedented: 14 billion barrels of oil, enough for 10 million households every day.

Here's my point. Their belief, matched with the right materials and resolve, produced a miracle. Reader, perhaps this book introduces new sand into your everyday project. Your walk in the Spirit, combined with resolve, just might become a miracle of your own.

Whoever said the Christian life is boring was doing it wrong. This is an adventure, one worth preoccupation and striving. But the thing is, an SMG needs to act like one in order to receive what is hoped for.

ACKNOWLEDGMENTS

This book took six months to write but thirty years to learn. My path from writing to readiness for a reader was smoothed by several good-willed and capable people.

My thanks to Rev. Joe Wenger, district superintendent for the Missionary Church, who nurtures a large network of leaders, both clergy and lay, toward stewarding the mysteries of God, and who was the first to show me 1 Corinthians 4:1, the hook for this book, in our idle conversation during a break at a board meeting.

Also, my thanks to three content reviewers who sharpened my thinking behind the writing: Dr. David McCabe, endowed professor of biblical theology and a New Testament expert, helped me discover incomplete ideas or unintended errors of language; Randy Lehman, chairman of the board of trustees for Bethel University and top 5 percent wealth manager for Northwestern Mutual, assessed accuracy and appropriateness of institutional narratives in the book; Kory Lantz represented target readers for me, scanning for confusing paragraphs and desirable but omitted content. He is executive director of Transformation Ministries in South Bend, Indiana, an after-school mentorship organization for underprivileged teens, and he is also an entrepreneur of several for-profit businesses to fund ministry.

Meanwhile, thanks to the colleagues with whom I work most directly every week, who advanced my thinking for this book during a multi-month devotional series embedded in our work meetings. Each of them is skilled as a project manager and steward of mysteries: Drs. Barb Bellefeuille, Shawn Holtgren, Terry Elam, and Misters Jerry White and Matt Lentsch.

Thank you to the Garvin Family Foundation for so believing this book could help faith integrate the workplace that they generously funded a large quantity of free copies for distribution to current and emerging leaders all across the country.

Finally, hi, Tammy. I see you—wink. Reader, she is my wife, but more. Tammy never complains when I keep thrusting myself into new projects that sometimes disrupt her life. Tammy, for more than thirty years, you have said dozens of smaller yeses after the biggest yes of all to that black velvet box cracked open in my hand. You roll with me, Ferris Wheel Wife.

> While strolling through the carnival life
> I found myself a Ferris Wheel Wife
> This gal, not most, is up for the challenge
> Of rising and falling an adventure's imbalance
>
> Grad school or ministry or move to Korea? "Sure!"
> Our chair swings swiftly in joyous detour
> Farmhouse or city, rich or poor
> "Move here!" "Try that!" That's my *amour*
>
> Whirly wheel spins dizzying revolution
> Our thirty-two cycles look kinda Dr. Seussian
> We flitter-tom-doodle, we saber-tom-toll
> But Wheel Wife chimes in, "That's how we roll!"
>
> Strap in, grip on, first forward then up
> You, feeler, front me, thinker, clinking "cheers!" on my cup
> Wheel forward, then up, even down hand in hand
> You always face forward with your Ferris Wheel Man

NOTES

Chapter 1: Steward the Mysteries

1. Craig S. Keener, *The Mind of the Spirit: Paul's Approach to Transformed Thinking* (Grand Rapids: Baker Academic, 2016), 259.

2. Stephen Miller, "Bald, Blind, and Single? Answers to Some of the Most Puzzling Questions about the Apostle Paul," *Christian History* #47, 1995, https://www.christianitytoday.com/history/issues/issue-47/bald-blind-single.html.

3. Jerry L. Sumney, *Steward of God's Mysteries: Paul and Early Church Tradition* (Grand Rapids: William B. Eerdmans Publishing Company, 2017), 170–173.

4. A. W. Tozer, *The Knowledge of the Holy: The Attributes of God, Their Meaning in the Christian Life* (New York: Harper & Row, 1961).

5. Philip W. Eaton, *Engaging the Culture, Changing the World: The Christian University in a Post-Christian World* (Downers Grove, IL: InterVarsity Press, 2011), 107.

6. Henry T. and Richard Blackaby, *Hearing God's Voice* (Nashville: B&H Publishing Group, 2002), 18.

7. Justin Taylor, "An FAQ on Mysticism and the Christian Life," *The Gospel Coalition*, October 30, 2015, https://www.thegospelcoalition.org/blogs/justin-taylor/an-faq-on-mysticism-and-the-christian-life/.

8. See the blog post by Kate Eby, "Demystifying the 5 Phases of Project Management," Smartsheet, https://www.smartsheet.com/blog/demystifying-5-phases-project-management. Or visit pmi.org to learn more about the Project Management Institute.

Chapter 2: Watching for Signs of Change

1. John and Donna Avant, *Yes Changes Everything: Opening the Door to Spiritual Transformation* (Buchanan, MI: Life Action Incorporated, 2020), 35.

2. Keener, *The Mind of the Spirit*, 114, 199.

3. C. S. Lewis, *Miracles* (1947), in *The Complete C. S. Lewis Signature Classics* (San Francisco: HarperSanFrancisco, 2002), 419.

4. Lewis, *Miracles* in *Signature Classics*, 422.

5. Leonard Sweet, *Nudge: Awakening Each Other to the God Who's Already There* (Colorado Springs: David C. Cook, 2010).

6. Ruth Haley Barton, *Pursuing God's Will Together: A Discernment Practice for Leadership Groups*, (Downers Grove, IL: IVP Books, 2012), 76.

7. John Piper, "Are Signs and Wonders for Today?" *Desiring God*, February 25, 1990, https://www.desiringgod.org/messages/are-signs-and-wonders-for-today.

8. Barton, *Pursuing God's Will Together*.

Chapter 3: When to Start (The Timing of God)

1. The Weather Channel, "Bus Photobombs The Weather Channel's Stream of Georgia Dome Implosion," November 20, 2017, https://www.youtube.com /watch?v=3oXhLdeuxDw&feature=youtu.be.

2. Bill Gross, "The Single Biggest Reason Why Start-Ups Succeed," TED Talk in Vancouver, BC, March 2015, https://www.youtube.com/watch?v=bNpx7gpSqbY& feature=youtu.be.

3. "10 Hardest Things to Do in Sports," *USA Today*, May 20, 2005, http://usato day30.usatoday.com/sports/ten-hardest-splash.htm.

4. "Finding the Perfect Pace for Product Launches," *Harvard Business Review*, Ju-ly-August 2018, https://hbr.org/2018/07/finding-the-perfect-pace-for-product-launches.

5. Sy Harding, "Has Warren Buffett Nailed Another Market Top?" *Forbes*, September 20, 2013, https://www.forbes.com/sites/sharding/2013/09/20/has-warren-buf fett-nailed-another-market-top/?sh=74cc9b2633af.

6. Stuart Albert, *When: The Art of Perfect Timing* (San Francisco: Jossey-Bass, 2013), 80.

7. Joyce Meyer, "What To Do When You're Waiting on God," *Everyday Answers with Joyce Meyer*, Joyce Meyer Ministries, https://joycemeyer.org/everydayanswers /ea-teachings/what-to-do-when-youre-waiting-on-god.

8. See also, Joyce Meyer, "When God's Timing Is Taking Too Long," *Everyday Answers with Joyce Meyer*, Joyce Meyer Ministries, https://joycemeyer.org/everydayan-swers/ea-teachings/when-gods-timing-is-taking-too-long.

9. Cindi McMenamin, "3 Ways to Be Sure an 'Open Door' Is from God," *Cross-walk*, https://www.ibelieve.com/faith/3-ways-to-be-sure-an-open-door-is-from-god. html.

10. Henry T. and Richard Blackaby, *Spiritual Leadership: Moving People on to God's Agenda, Revised & Expanded* (Nashville: B & H Publishing Group, 2011), 22.

11. John P. Kotter, *A Sense of Urgency* (Boston: Harvard Business Press, 2008), 8.

12. Keener, *The Mind of the Spirit*, 7.

13. Malcom Gladwell, *Blink: The Power of Thinking without Thinking* (New York: Little, Brown and Company, 2005), 52.

14. Gladwell, *Blink*, 136.

15. Leonard Mlodinow, *Elastic: Unlocking Your Brain's Ability to Embrace Change* (New York: Vintage Books, 2018).

16. Daniel Kahneman, *Thinking, Fast and Slow* (New York: Farrar, Straus and Giroux, 2011).

Chapter 4: Accomplices You Didn't Recruit

1. Mark Batterson and Richard Foth, with Susanna Foth Aughtmon, *A Trip around the Sun: Turning Your Everyday Life into the Adventure of a Lifetime* (Grand Rapids: Baker Books, 2015), 36.

2. Felix Just, "Paul's Associates and Co-Workers," E.N.T.E.R.: Electronic New Testament Educational Resources, January 10, 2013, https://catholic-resources.org /Bible/Pauline_Associates.htm.

3. Os Guinness, *The Call: Finding and Fulfilling the Central Purpose of Your Life* (Nashville: Word Publishing, 1998).

4. Camila Domonoske, "Musician Wins $260,000 in Lawsuit against Ex-Girlfriend Who Sabotaged Career," NPR, June 15, 2018, https://www.npr .org/2018/06/15/620202403/musician-wins-260-000-in-lawsuit-against-ex-girl friend-who-sabotaged-career#:~:text=Live%20Sessions-,Musician%20Wins%20 %24260%2C000%20In%20Lawsuit%20Against%20Ex%2DGirlfriend%20 Who%20Sabotaged,sent%20him%20a%20fake%20rejection.

5. Kenneth Berding, *What Are Spiritual Gifts? Rethinking the Conventional View* (Grand Rapids: Kregel Publications, 2007).

6. This list and paraphrased explanations come from Jeff Carver, "Spiritual Gifts: Definitions and Descriptions," https://spiritualgiftstest.com/spiritual-gifts/.

7. Ed Catmull with Amy Wallace, *Creativity, Inc.: Overcoming the Unseen Forces That Stand in the Way of True Inspiration* (New York: Random House, 2014), 91, 98, 111.

8. George Barna, *The Power of Team Leadership: Finding Strength in Shared Responsibility* (Colorado Springs: Waterbrook Press, 2001), 33.

9. Sarah Miller Caldicott, *Midnight Lunch: The 4 Phases of Team Collaboration Success from Thomas Edison's Lab* (Hoboken, NJ: John Wiley & Sons, 2013), 36.

10. Brene Brown, *Daring Greatly: How the Courage to Be Vulnerable Transforms the Way We Live, Love, Parent, and Lead* (New York: Penguin Publishing Group, 2012), 65.

11. Brown, *Daring Greatly*, 198.

12. Brown, *Daring Greatly*, 211.

13. Brown, *Daring Greatly*, 27.

14. Barton, *Pursuing God's Will Together*, 98–99.

Chapter 5: God Rewards Financial Integrity

1. Terry T. Munday, *It's Not about the Money: How to Tap into God-Given Generosity* (Oklahoma City: TQL Press, 2009), 24.

2. Henri J. M. Nouwen, *A Spirituality of Fundraising* (Nashville: Upper Room Books, 2011), 31.

3. Andy Stanley, *How to be Rich: It's Not What You Have. It's What You Do with What You Have* (Grand Rapids: Zondervan, 2013), 39.

4. Stanley, *How to Be Rich*, 102.

5. Martin Luther, "The Distinction between the Law and the Gospel," January 1, 1532, trans. Willard L. Burce, *Concordia Journal* (April 1992), http://www.ccle.org/wp-content/uploads/2013/07/LutherSermon.pdf, 153.

6. Luther, "The Distinction," 156–58.

7. David Croteau (ed.), Bobby Eklund, Ken Hemphill, Reggie Kidd, Gary North, Scott Preissler, *Perspectives on Tithing: Four Views*, (Nashville: Bolderman & Holman, 2011).

8. Philip Graham Ryken, *Written in Stone: The Ten Commandments and Today's Moral Crisis* (Philipsburg, NJ: P & R Publishing, 2010), 174.

9. Ryken, *Written in Stone*, 181.

10. A. W. Tozer, *The Purpose of Man*, in *The Essential Tozer Collection*, ed. James L. Snyder (Bloomington, MN: Bethany House, 2017), 31.

11. Nassim Nicholas Taleb, *Skin in the Game: Hidden Asymmetries in Daily Life* (New York: Random House, 2018).

12. Blackaby and Blackaby, *Spiritual Leadership*, 97.

13. Jonathan Haidt, *The Righteous Mind: Why Good People Are Divided by Politics and Religion* (New York: Vintage Books, 2012), 310.

14. R. Mark Dillon, *Giving and Getting in the Kingdom: A Field Guide* (Chicago: Moody Publishers, 2012), 19.

15. Eli Broad with Swati Pandey, *The Art of Being Unreasonable: Lessons in Unconventional Thinking* (Hoboken, NJ: John Wiley & Sons, Inc., 2012), 138.

Chapter 6: Confrontation, Not Avoidance, Brings Peace

1. Kerry Patterson, Joseph Grenny, Ron McMillan, and Al Switler, *Crucial Conversations: Tools for Talking When Stakes Are High*, 2nd ed. (New York: McGraw-Hill, 2012), 51–52.

2. Stephen M. R. Covey with Rebecca R. Merrill, *The Speed of Trust: The One Thing That Changes Everything* (New York: Free Press, 2006).

3. Rick Sorensen, "The Lord's Anger: 4 Times Jesus Did Not 'Turn the Other Cheek,'" *Crosswalk*, September 25, 2018, https://www.crosswalk.com/faith/bible-study/the-lord-s-anger-4-times-jesus-did-not-turn-the-other-cheek.html.

4. Haidt, *The Righteous Mind*, 29.

5. Gregg Chenoweth, *Nonprofit and For-Profit Workers during Organizational Innovation: Psychological Contract, Uncertainty, and Communication Coping Tactics*, unpublished doctoral dissertation (Detroit: Wayne State University, 2003).

6. D. Michael Lindsay with M. G. Hager, *View From the Top: An Inside Look at How People in Power See and Shape the World* (Hoboken, NJ: John Wiley & Sons, Inc., 2014).

7. Archie Brown, *The Myth of the Strong Leader: Political Leadership in the Modern Age* (New York: Basic Books, 2014), 349.

8. Patterson, Grenny, McMillan, and Switler, *Crucial Conversations*.

9. Roger Fisher, William Ury, and Bruce Patton, *Getting to Yes: Negotiating Agreement without Giving In* (New York: Penguin Books, 1981).

10. Peter Scazzero, *The Emotionally Healthy Leader: How Transforming Your Inner Life Will Deeply Transform Your Church, Team, and the World* (Grand Rapids: Zondervan, 2015), 188.

Chapter 7: Pleased by Pain

1. A. J. Swoboda, *A Glorious Dark: Finding Hope in the Tension between Belief and Experience* (Grand Rapids: BakerBooks, 2014).

2. Dr. Archibald D. Hart, *The Hidden Link between Adrenaline and Stress: The Exciting New Breakthrough That Helps You Overcome Stress Damage* (Nashville: Thomas Nelson, 1995), 49.

3. William Lane Craig and Chad Meister, eds, *God Is Great, God Is Good: Why Believing in God Is Reasonable and Responsible* (Downers Grove, IL: IVP Books, 2009), 108.

4. David Brooks, *The Road to Character* (New York: Random House, 2015), 95, 94.

5. T. D. Jakes, *Crushing: God Turns Pressure into Power* (Nashville: FaithWords, 2019), 94.

6. Barry C. Black, *The Blessing of Adversity: Finding Your God-Given Purpose in Life's Troubles* (Carol Stream, IL: Tyndale House, 2011).

7. Jon Bloom, "Why You Have That Thorn," *Desiring God*, April 13, 2018, https://www.desiringgod.org/articles/why-you-have-that-thorn.

8. Thomas Gilovich and Lee Ross, *The Wisest One in the Room: How You Can Benefit From Social Psychology's Most Powerful Insights* (New York: Free Press, 2015), 166–67.

9. Alan Kreider, *The Patient Ferment of the Early Church: The Improbable Rise of Christianity in the Roman Empire* (Grand Rapids: Baker Academic, 2016).

10. Robert J. Morgan, *The Red Sea Rules: 10 God-Given Strategies for Difficult Times* (Nashville: W Publishing, 2014), 6.

11. Morgan, *Red Sea Rules*, 69.

12. Eric Metaxas, *Bonhoeffer: Pastor, Martyr, Prophet, Spy* (Nashville: Thomas Nelson, 2010), 495.

13. Michael Wear, *Reclaiming Hope: Lessons Learned in the Obama White House about the Future of Faith in America* (Nashville: Thomas Nelson, 2017), 192.

Chapter 8: Bear Witness to Christ as You Go

1. Josh Bersin, "The Rise of the Social Enterprise: A New Paradigm for Business," *Forbes*, April 3, 2018, https://www.forbes.com/sites/joshbersin/2018/04/03/the-rise-of-the-social-enterprise-a-new-paradigm-for-business/?sh=51c19efb71f0.

2. John Zogby, *The Way We'll Be: The Zogby Report on the Transformation of the American Dream* (New York: Random House, 2008), 121, 125, 129.

3. John Arnold Schmalzbauer and Kathleen A. Mahoney, *The Resilience of Religion in American Higher Education* (Waco, TX: Baylor University Press, 2018).

4. Richard S. Taylor, *A Right Conception of Sin: Its Relation to Right Thinking and Right Living*, rev. ed. (Kansas City, MO: Beacon Hill Press, 1945), 16.

5. Dr. Art Lindsley, "The Priesthood of All Believers," Institute for Faith, Work, and Economics, October 15, 2013, https://tifwe.org/resource/the-priesthood-of-all-believers/.

6. James K. A. Smith, *Desiring the Kingdom: Worship, Worldview, and Cultural Formation, Cultural Liturgies vol. 1* (Grand Rapids: Baker Academic, 2009), 69–70.

7. Robert E. Coleman, *The Master Plan of Evangelism* (Grand Rapids: Fleming H. Revell, 1964).

8. Elmer L. Towns and Douglas Porter, *The Ten Greatest Revivals Ever* (Ventura, CA: Gospel Light Publications, 2004).

9. Towns and Porter, 123.

10. Towns and Porter, 119.

11. Towns and Porter, 156.

12. Towns and Porter, 213-15.